DEAR SON

VINCENT

ISBN 979-8-89243-287-0 (paperback)
ISBN 979-8-89243-288-7 (digital)

Christian Faith Publishing
832 Park Avenue
Meadville, PA 16335
www.christianfaithpublishing.com

Printed in the United States of America

LETTER I

Dear Son,

What does a father say to a son when it is his time to go out on his own? The world is so huge. The possibilities endless. Yet the root of it all is pretty much the same. I know because I was eighteen once…I'm surprised that you stayed as long as you did. I was eighteen, and I wanted to try it all, experience everything. I assumed everything was enough to satisfy me. It wasn't. I always wanted more. Life is designed that way. It is meant to keep you searching until you understand deep in your heart what this life is for. You will find that it is not what you think it is. Life will never satisfy you if you let the world or any of its stuff guide the flame within your heart. You will always wind up feeling unsatisfied and never quite full. Trust me, I've been there too. I was the one that went far off the well-beaten path. I got way too deep in the bushes, completely lost. Unless you stick to the lakes and the rivers that you are used to, you will too.

Life is brimming with all types of people. The great majority are just passing through for a very short moment in your life. Do not follow them. Do not pick up their ways.

You were given a mind to think for yourself. You were taught the right thing to do, and you have your feet to make your own way. Make sure you place them in the proper order! If you make your own way but do the wrong thing, then you will end up at the wrong place. If you do the right thing, then you will always be in the right place.

I do not need to remind you that the man writing this has a history of learning life's lessons the hard way. Learning things the hard way gets the lesson deep in your soul. Too deep and a man becomes bitter. Not enough and he never quite learns. My biggest prayer for you is that you learn fast and learn early in your life. You will gain the most success if you are obedient to God. Out of your obedience will come wisdom that keeps you from making foolish choices while also having the ability to face life's challenges. Always look to your Bible for answers before asking others. The Bible is better than any book on the "bestseller" list. In fact, it has been printed with exponential growth and read by countless more people than any book in the history of man. The knowledge and wisdom from the Bible have withstood the test of time, and it will be around long after you are gone from this world. When it is time to pass something down to your own kids, teaching them to get answers from their Bible will have greater impact on their entire lives than anything. If you open it up, you will see no mention of what college you should go to or what type of job you should get. You will find plenty of golden wisdom that is designed to bring out the best in you no matter what season of life you are going through. It is written to make you into a golden person with a golden heart. Having a golden heart will get you to the dinner table with people on every rung of the ladder. You will be treated warmly, and it will always feel right. That is the key to a good life. It's all about relationships.

The Bible is also written from the same loving spirit that your own father is writing this letter to you. I want only the best for you, son. I speak from the wellspring of love deep in my heart. You will probably not understand until you have your own children, and the circle of love is complete. As a father, I know that depending on where you are at in your heart, my words can have a variety of impact on you. Although some parts of the letter may convict you, my goal is never to convict. Your own heart will do that in its own time. My goal is to get you to see yourself the way that your mother and I see you: as exceptionally gifted, with more tools and talent than you even know you have. You are not a regular kid. You are special. When you look at yourself in the mirror, I want you to know that in your mind, to feel it in your heart, and to believe it with every bit of your spirit. When you get to that stage, you will live life to your fullest potential.

Love,
Dad

LETTER 2

Dear Son,

Many are the plans in a person's heart, but it is the Lord's purpose that prevails (Proverbs 19:21). I've thought so much about what to say to you, words of blessing over your life—words that I can speak over your life that imprint themselves into your mind and establish themselves into your heart so that your beliefs are rooted in the truth of who you are. Your beliefs will lead you no matter the circumstance. They are the lens through which you interpret and respond to the world. If they are right, then no man, under any circumstance, will ever steal your cup of joy. If they are right, then you will find value in situations that are unfair. If they are right, then you will be successful if you do not achieve your goal even if it means you fail seventy times seven times. Having the right beliefs is what makes you understand when justice must be served even when it is you or somebody that you love that must pay. Having the right beliefs keep you humble so that success does not cause you to be proud. Nobody likes being around a proud person. Having the right beliefs is what makes a man determined enough to never quit. Having the right beliefs is a key ingredient to achieving your goals while also having a cup that runneth over.

In direct and equal proportion, having the wrong beliefs can have devastating consequences over your life. Having the wrong beliefs make a man quit before he ever knows what he is even made of. Having the wrong beliefs can put you down a path that you might not recover from. Having the wrong beliefs will cause you to live with contradictions and confusion in your life. My biggest prayer for you is that God bless you with the knowledge of the truth so that your own beliefs are in line with His purpose for your life. His purpose for your life is between you and Him. While it may affect what happens between you and other people, it is only between you and God. It is your first order of business that often gets pushed to the last. It is the one most directly in front of you, the most obvious. Stubbornness will keep you from seeing it. The sooner you learn and perceive and actually commit to your purpose, the sooner your heart will be content, and the feeling of being a restless wanderer will be gone. May God bless you with that gift so that you don't waste too many years. There is nothing more difficult to overcome than a late start. If you do start late, always learn everything you can, every chance you get, from every situation you have. Oftentimes, the seemingly inconsequential circumstance is what turns out to be your saving grace. The monotonous, boring season of your life becomes the season that shapes you the most. How you respond will impact how the world responds to you. How you respond will be caused by how you see yourself in the mirror. The two are intertwined and cannot be separated.

If you respond to a situation well, then you will be rewarded well. There will be times when it will feel like you are not being rewarded fairly. You may feel stuck while others get ahead. Remember, you are working for God, so your reward will come from God. No man can pay you what you are actually worth because you are a priceless vessel of God. Your reward comes from heaven. God has a way to make the man who lives in a tent feels like he has more riches than the man who lives in a mansion. Do not be so shallow that you make the mansion your goal. Respond well by doing the right thing, and God, who owns the cattle and all the hills, has a way to shower His favor upon your life. And you will know what true riches are. True riches are to know the intrinsic value of yourself and others no matter where either of you lies on the social ladder. True riches come from the things that do not have a price tag. True riches are what you get when your beliefs are such that you value the stuff that brought you joy when you were a child. Do not let the world deceive you into thinking that it, or any of its products, holds the magic key for you to have true riches. True riches will make your cup of joy runneth over.

Joy is much greater than happiness. Joy is something you feel way down in your spirit. It lasts a long, long time. My guess is that joy is eternal. Happiness is not. Happiness is a nice thing, but happiness is fleeting. Happiness is superficial. It depends on things outside of you. It can be dressed up and faked, like a smile and a hello from somebody who could care less to see you. Joy is something you are born with. It is why when you were a baby, every morning and most of the day, your eyes were baby wide, and you smiled for no apparent reason. Remember this and understand what this means, son: you were born naked. You had no phone. You had no friends. You had no girlfriend. You had no parties. You had no favorite sports team. You had no car. You had no mansion. You had no plans for a vacation. You had no status, yet by the strength of your being innocent and pure and filled with joy, you were the most attractive person in the room. You had the most minimal necessities, yet you had joy. Pay attention to what I am saying: Everything that brings you joy comes from within. You were born with it. When your life leads you down a path so that you begin to believe that you need anything from this world to be happy or joyful or free, then your beliefs are wrong, and you need to self-correct, or you will end up lost. It's a sad thing, but most of the world is lost.

Love,
Dad

LETTER 3

Dear Son,

Sad thing, the bulk of the world is lost. Have you ever wondered how a goose can find its way over two thousand miles, despite every obstacle, to a place it has never seen? And it can do this even if it gets separated from the flock. The reason why is because it knows its purpose without thinking about its purpose. It lives its purpose every day without becoming distracted. It always stays aligned with its True North. All creatures have a True North. There are no animals that intentionally kill themselves because they all stay aligned with their True North. You have a True North. Your True North never changes. For humans, it is the place where morality and meaning intersect. It is the place where who you are is intrinsically aligned with God's will and purpose for your life.

If you always do the right thing, you will always be going in the right direction, and your life will have its true meaning. This is not to say that it will always be comfortable, even a goose encounters bad weather. Sometimes, after going through a storm, it may even feel like you are completely lost. True North will get you back to your bearings. It will always lead you to a paradise where life and riches are found in abundance. Remember, to have life is to have good physical, emotional, and spiritual health; riches are things that you cannot buy.

The compass for True North is found in your heart. You were born with it. You received it as a gift and inheritance from God. It is aligned with something you cannot see. In the same way that a compass always points north so does your heart. It is drawn by God. Be aware that there is a thing that can interfere with a compass which causes it to give a false reading. It is called a magnet. This only happens when the magnet is allowed to get too close to the compass. The magnet has a very strong attractive force, but if you keep the magnet away from the compass, it will not interfere with the natural reading. If the compass is your heart, the magnet can be anything that causes you to be misled and distracted from your True North. You must realize the importance of keeping the magnets far away from the compass. If you do, you will never lose your way. You will make the most of your life. You will live your best life.

My hope and prayer for you is that you make the most of your life so that you can live your best life. Do not be deceived. Your best life is not lived on the stage of a social media platform. It is not on Facebook, Instagram, or TikTok. The vast majority of the people on your friend list will not show up when the chips are down. Their opinion does not matter. What they think of you has no bearing on your life. Do not allow them too close to your compass. They are magnets. They will take you way off your True North. They will lead you astray. They will misguide you, and when you end up lost, they will be nowhere around.

When you find yourself lost, you will likely be alone. Be still. Pray. And wait on God. Do not reach out to the same lost people that helped you get lost in the first place. To be separated from them is a good thing. Look to your Bible for answers. The first verse in the book of Psalms says, "Blessed is he who does not walk in step with the wicked." In other words, out of your lostness came separation. Your separation may feel lonely at first, but it is actually a blessing because it is keeping you from the magnet that caused you to lose your way. Your separation is a great gift because it forces you to stand on your own. Standing on your own is when you get autonomy. Autonomy plus responsibility are the first two steps to becoming a man.

Ultimately, this is what these letters are all about. These letters are written to help you become a man. They are intended to help you to be the best version of yourself. To dig deep and find the real you. To prepare you so that you are armed and ready to fight your greatest battle, which is a battle that comes from within. Within every man are two wolves. The one that rules is the one you feed the most. Have caution here because the magnets often feed the worst wolf. You are responsible over what each wolf gets fed, how often it is fed, and by whom. If a shady person feeds it, then it is inclined to overlook the shady character for the food. A burglar once said, "The easiest way to get past a big dog is to feed it." This is a pretty simple technique, but this is how riches are stolen. If you allow the burglar (Satan) to feed the wolf within you, your riches will be stolen.

Love,
Dad

LETTER 4

Dear Son,

You were born alone, and you will die alone. You have made it this far without needing any of the people you are around, and you will make it through the rest of your life when they are gone. You will do well to know in your heart that the bulk of the everyday faces are just passing through your life, even the ones you spend most of your time with. They will be in and out just like a fad. Some may even pop up later. You will be fine when they go. This is not meant to be a cynical letter; it comes from a deep well of experience—experience that includes the wrong belief that people who did not have their own lives together could help me with mine. Experience that truly understands how much bad choices, like choosing bad friends, cost a man.

A bad friend is not necessarily a bad person; it just means that you and the bad friend make a bad combination. Oxygen is safe when it is alone but place it with acetylene and it becomes highly explosive. The rule of synergy also applies. Synergy is when the energy of two works together to exponentially increase a workload. If you can pull forty pounds and I can pull forty pounds, together, we can pull much more than eighty pounds because of synergy. The same thing happens for destructive behavior. Bad behavior feeds bad behavior. You and the "bad" friend make a bad combination because ideas are more likely to become a reality in the hands of two people. In fact, they are at least twice as likely to become a reality in the hands of two people.

This is why it is so important that you learn to stand on your own. Standing on your own means that you are able to make responsible choices while also paying for the consequences of irresponsible choices. Standing on your own pushes you up. It makes your back and shoulders strong. It stretches you. It shows you your capability. It forces you to be responsible for your choices. If you are honest to yourself, win or lose, you get all the credit. If you get all the credit and you lose, then it keeps you humble. If you get all the credit and you win, it helps you believe in yourself. They call that growing up.

Both are valuable because you learn from both. They balance each other out until, one day, you will reach the age where experience has taught you to make wise choices. At this stage, you will get ahead. Wise choices always have the best long-term consequences for all people involved. Wise choices are not always the most pleasurable choices. If you make choices based on pleasure, then you will become a slave to pleasure. Being a slave means that you are not your own man.

Wise choices are choices that are grounded on principle. It takes character to make wise choices. In a nutshell, character is who you are when nobody is looking. Wise choices have little to do with immediate financial gain. When you make wise choices consistently, your entire life will blossom. It will begin to flourish like a forest along the river. You will gain God's blessings and riches. Wisdom is one of God's riches. Remember, riches are those things that you cannot buy.

God's riches are a blessing to you that God uses to bless others through you. That means you cannot hide them away. Like all the riches you cannot buy, they are meant to be scattered. Give them away freely, son. Ironically, the more you give, the more you will receive. The more seeds that a farmer plants, the more fruit he receives. It is one of God's spiritual laws that is patterned after his natural laws.

Love,
Dad

LETTER 5

Dear Son,

Only God can make you whole. The greatest human folly is to believe that there is something in the physical realm that can make man whole. That is impossible because man is made of more than the physical body. Man is a combination of his body, mind, and spirit. Generally, especially in the westernized society you were raised into, man is thought of in that order: body, mind, spirit. He constructs his life in that order. He nourishes himself in the order. He creates his values in that order. His self-esteem is created in that order. And the doctor even fixes him in that order.

This is backward. It causes a superficial worldview, which is to say a shallow view of the world. Since he is in the world, it also causes a shallow view of himself. Shallowness on the inside equates to shallowness on the outside. There is very little life that is able to survive in a shallow body of water. That's no good because man is made up of mostly water. Man thinks of his life in terms of what he can perceive through the senses. This causes him to be shallow and easy to distract. You will be an easy target for Satan if you see yourself in the shallow, empty terms the world uses to define you. If you let your heart find value in any single thing you can buy, then you are doomed to slavery.

Kingdoms are built on the backs of men. The world is Satan's kingdom. Satan needs slaves to build his kingdom. You were not born a slave. Do not sell yourself off at a slave auction. The minute you buy into the belief that your wholeness comes from the world, then you have bought into a lie. Believing a lie causes confusion. Believing a lie causes you to be misguided and lost. Lies are magnets.

How can a thing in the physical realm complete a thing in the spiritual? It cannot! The essence of who you are is spiritual. Fill that first. If something happens to your body, it is the spirit that keeps you keeping on. It is the spirit that fills you with life. The spirit is supernaturally shaped by reading God's Word, prayer, and fasting. Practice these three. Learn them well, and you shall live well. Most importantly, if you are ever struggling, work on these first. Struggle generally develops in the heart. The heart directly effects and affects the spirit. Reading your Bible, praying, and fasting bring peace to the heart. The Bible says, "A heart at peace gives life to the body." When a person is stressed out (not at peace), their body releases a hormone called cortisol. Too much cortisol over a longer period of time causes a whole lot of major health issues. The Bible was telling people this exact thing without explaining the science behind it, and it has taken science three thousand years to figure it out. Your Bible was right all along. Keep in mind your Bible is not a science book; if it was, it would be out of date every hundred years.

The Bible deals with spiritual laws that undoubtedly affect the spirit. If you are feeling lost or empty inside, look here first. The world's design is meant so that you are not able to violate nature's laws. Nature has laws so that the world is systematically consistent. You do not get a choice whether or not you want to follow these laws. All people must follow these laws. We, humans, base scientific research and scientific study on these laws. They are necessary for life on earth to continue. For example, without the law of gravity, you would float out into space.

The spirit also has laws. The laws of the spirit are less obvious. You cannot see them, but you do experience their physical effects. The spiritual laws may not even be as apparently necessary, but they are. You do get a choice on whether or not you want to follow these laws. If you obey them, then you will live well. If others disobey them and it affects you, then you should adjust with grace. If every person obeys the spiritual laws, there will be peace. Obeying the laws of the spirit will help you to gain riches that money cannot buy. You will prosper greatly by obeying these laws. The government is not able to tax this type of prosperity. Even better the riches gained through the spirit are the only way for you to feel whole and complete. All else that you have gained in your life will pass away and be forgotten. The riches gained by the spirit have eternal value, lasting forever.

As you go off into the world and make your own way, you will do well to learn how to feed and nourish your spirit first. There is an inverse principle that works like the root system of a tree. The deeper and more well-established the root system, the better a tree is able to withstand a storm. The root is the part of the tree that you cannot see. It searches deep places. It searches for water and nutrients to sustain life for itself. Think of the root as your spirit. Strong roots make the tree healthy. When a tree is healthy, all life is blessed through it. A tree provides shelter, and it produces seeds. It even purifies the toxic air and returns healthy air. And it does it all for free.

Are you beginning to see the pattern? The riches that have the most value are those you cannot buy. They are not meant to be stored away or sold. They are meant to satisfy, to make you complete, to enjoy, to give you life, and then paid forward to others.

Love,
Dad

LETTER 6

Dear Son,

The most valuable thing that you possess is your voice. It is made up of a compilation of tools that you have within you. Your voice is the fingerprint of who you are. It is more than the "thing that got deeper" when you turned fifteen. The voice box that got deeper is a physical representation of you. It is a sound maker and identity marker that is specific to you, but it is only a part of you. Just like your body only represents the part we can all see, there is more to you than that. So too, your voice represents the inner, deeper you.

The tongue and the sounds it makes represent your voice. It is the hardest part to tame because it is the part that speaks for the heart. The heart is made up of the fabric of who you are.

The threads of that fabric are so tightly woven that it would be near impossible to break them down in a letter. I will stay to the edges. People are complicated. There are thousands of threads that make them up. Some of those threads are metaphysical; some are physical (brain chemicals), and some are a part of you because of the life experiences that you've been through. Many do not even seem to fit together; we could call that a mystery. Collectively those threads are your voice. They are a fingerprint of your soul and spirit. They are deeply influenced by your internal belief system which influences how you perceive the world. Your voice always displays the real you. Are you kind or cruel? Are you compassionate or callous? Are you loud and arrogant, or are you quiet and confident? The signature of your voice is written by what you say and how you act. Your actions speak volumes, oftentimes, without even saying a word. Your voice is how the people who know you will always remember you. It is how you have expressed yourself throughout your life.

The language you use, the words you say, are pushed out by the breath within you. In the Bible, man is just bones until God blows His breath in Him. The breath is inseparable from life. Your words are a mixture of your thoughts, ideas, and beliefs coded with your breath (air) to make sound vibrations. That is how you communicate your thoughts, ideas, and beliefs. Communication is how you express yourself. It is your song to the world. Self-expression is a fundamental part of your life. To live your best life, you must learn to express the real you. That means you will have to learn who you really are. That happens with experience and testing and staying away from magnets.

The best way to learn who a person is, is to listen to their voice. Even better, listen to what they say, and then watch what they do. If their actions do not line up with their words, be suspicious. Do not be naive. When the word spoken does not line up with what you see, it is a lie. They are torn between what they say and what they mean. Their real voice does not line up with their tongue. You could say, their song is out of harmony.

Son, I pray for you all the time. Daily. I pray that you find your voice early, that you trust your voice, and that you take care to use your voice for the right purpose. I pray your voice is a mirror reflection of God. Live an honest life. Speak the truth. Sometimes, that will require boldness. Together, truth told with boldness is a work of the spirit. They are two threads of the fabric of your voice. Speaking the truth will put you at odds with the world. Say the truth anyway because unless you learn to say the truth, you will always feel the anxiety that comes from not living your real purpose.

Your purpose is not something that I chose for you. It is not something that you get to choose either. It was designed by God into your life. You must figure that out on your own. There are some general themes like glorifying God and worshiping God, but ultimately, your purpose is between you and God. That will take lots of prayer and study and reflection. No two people have the same purpose. We each have an individual purpose. Your voice is amplified when you use it in conjunction with your purpose. It is as if God gives you a megaphone to help you as long as you are using your voice for your life purpose. Your voice is one of the many riches you were born with. It is an important tool in your toolbox.

You must use your voice in alignment with the truth. There is no such thing as having our own truth. That would mean that there are billions of truths in the world, and that is impossible. That is a logical contradiction because truth by its nature is exclusive. There is only one truth. The difference is that there are many voices. What a person believes regarding the truth does not make it true. Just think: if we are both looking at the same color red, but I am color blind, so I see green; it does not mean there are two different colors. It means that I am missing some of the information, so I do not know the truth. The lesson for you is to understand this and use your voice wisely. The folly of youth is to use your voice when it is motivated by emotion without thinking through all sides of an argument in order to search out the truth. You will do your best to follow these three rules: read your Bible, meditate, and pray. The Holy Spirit will give you wise counsel. When you are on the right side of the truth, then use your voice and all the decibels necessary to be heard. Scream if you have to. Yell it from the rooftops. I am sure that if it is enough to still bring you to the rooftop to make your voice heard, then it is part of your life purpose. And your voice will be heard. God will make sure the people who are supposed to hear it do hear it.

Love,
Dad

LETTER 7

Dear Son,

Tools are talents, gifts, and abilities that you have. You would be amazed at all the tools you have. You were born with a full toolbox. You have to figure out all their different uses. That's part of growing up. You were handed your tools as a birthright. They were free. They are yours to use however you choose. They are yours so that you may construct your own life. Be careful because you can also use them to destroy your life or waste your life. Take care of them. They are yours to use, so do not just leave them there in the toolbox. Use them. Pull them out and study them. To use them or lose them is not really true. They will always be there. The more you use them, the handier you become with them. The more you practice, the more capable you become and the more self-confidence you gain.

Even during an entire lifetime, you will never reach your highest potential in all the areas of your life that you have tools for. You will learn that some tools have multiple uses, and some are very specific. It takes years of learning yourself to learn your tools. There have been many studies that say that it takes about ten thousand hours to master something. When you master something, you are using a combination of tools, each for their proper use. Mastering your tools will help you to master other things. Mastering your tools is one of the threads necessary to knowing yourself.

First thing you must learn is the habit of getting up and just showing up to work. This is a valuable habit that takes much self-will and commitment. Getting up and showing up does not mean that you leave the house to go get paid at a job. It means that you make a willful decision to engage your life. Hence you are showing up when you wake up and do more than go through the motions, being unengaged. I call it wasting your day. After committing yourself to the work, you will eventually learn how to position yourself and hold your tools for the best effect. You will gain confidence in yourself, and people will gain confidence in you. Showing up with your sleeves rolled up tells everybody, and yourself, that you are committed for the moment. As the calluses form so does proof that the commitment is part of you. Calluses show that you are committed for the long haul. Showing up is one step past "just talking about it." Showing up is the step before doing the work. Doing the work is necessary to find the resources. The resources are everywhere. You must learn what yours are in order to use them for the best results. There will be times when you cannot find the proper resources. That is when you must be resourceful and figure it out. Figuring it out is easier the more knowledge you gain. You gain knowledge by reading and learning from standing on the shoulders of those who went before you. This is all part of growing up.

You'll never find the resources unless you get the shovel out and start digging. The shovel is made up of solid wood, solid steel, and a fastener. They are a combination of resources that were once very crude. Somebody took them and shaped them so that they could be a useful tool. The shovel is one of your tools. It is useless until you pull it out of the shed and use it. It is made up of a combination of things you were born with that you probably do not even realize you have. You can liken it to hopeful determination, commitment, intention, and will. Like the shovel, they are useless unless you put them to work. They have no value as long as you keep them in the thoughts stage. You must place them behind an action. Better said, put them to work. If you put them to work, then you can build anything that your mind can imagine. In fact, your imagination is another tool. If you do not have immediate resources, you can use your tools to dig for more resources. Be creative. Creativity is another tool.

If you are not careful with your tools, then you will make a mess. How you choose to use your tools is directly related to your beliefs. This is why I told you that your beliefs are so important. A bad belief system is dangerous. You will ruin your life and the life of others if you use your tools in the wrong way. Think what could happen if a person used a hammer instead of a polish rag to clean a car? That might sound like an extreme analogy, but people use destructive language rather than constructive language on themselves and each other all the time. Bad language can have much worse consequences than using a hammer on a car. People use bad language in the form of lies and destructive thoughts to themselves in the mirror every day. The consequences for destructive language and destructive behavior are similar: both destroy lives. People are much more valuable than a car, and words are much more destructive than a hammer.

When you learn to use your shovel or any of your tools properly, then your tools will stay sharp and shiny. Polished. You might hear of a person who is "polished." That's because they have chosen to use their tools to the fullest.

Understand that you have many more tools than just a shovel. I could write you an entire series of books explaining all of your tools and their many uses. If I did that, it would take away from your life journey. Your tools are to be treasured. Treasures are meant to be searched out. They are meant to be looked for and found by you. If you are to live your best life, a part of that journey will be you searching for those treasures and learning to use them. When you find the hidden treasures within yourself, you will also see yourself as you are supposed to: as a person with intrinsic value and deep riches—riches you were born with. Riches you will always have no matter whose dinner table you sit at or what color robe you wear. But one important thing, son, you will never even be able to scratch the surface unless you use your tools. That takes putting the smart phone down for long periods so that you can learn who you really are.

You will not know unless you use your mirror. Your mirror is your tool for self-awareness. When you use it, make sure you use it under the light. The light will show you the truth. It will not allow any deception or flaw to be hidden. The light is the Word of God. It is meant to show you the truth about your tools and the proper uses of them. It is meant to show you who you are created to be. The light allows you to see your tools and use them for constructive purposes.

The first instructions from God to man are for constructive purposes: "Be fruitful and multiply. Subdue the earth." He is literally telling all of us to produce and make stuff. Take part in creation. Use your tools to build. Building takes place during the day, under the light. What construction crew do you know that works at night? Those that do work at night only do so as part of a strategy. Do your best to make the most of your day and remain in the light.

Use your tools to build yourself up, to build others up, and to build bridges. Bridges are connections between people. Bridges are safe when they are built on solid ground. They are okay when they are stable and well-maintained. You are responsible for the ground on which your side of the bridge is built. Responsibility is one of your tools. Learning this tool well is part of growing up.

Love,
Dad

LETTER 8

Dear Son,

There is a tool that you possess that represents the real you, and you must learn to master it. The tool that I am speaking of is your language. It is imperative that you master your ability to speak using the right language for the right setting with your heart in the right place. If you are unable to keep up in the conversation because the concepts are above your head, speak little. Do not try to sprinkle big words into a sentence to make yourself sound more educated than you are. That is a fool's mistake, and it will do more harm than good. It is wise general practice to speak less than you talk. After all, God did give you two ears and only one mouth. He is obviously saying listen twice as much as you talk. When you are in a setting with heathens, do not stoop down to the lower language that they are using. Do not cuss around men, women, children, and your elders. Cussing is the fastest way for people to learn which class of person you are. Class is not determined by how much money you make or what part of town you live in. Some of the classiest people come from the poorest part of town, and some of the lowest class people come from the wealthiest part of town. Class is a label you get from how you act. That's all.

"The tongue has no bone but can crush and kill a person."

If you have friends that do not cuss, then I would say that you have chosen your friends well. Just know that there is no grey area with God. Cussing is an outward expression of an inward cancer called sin. Hard language—which is language that glorifies crime, adultery, lasciviousness, debauchery, violence, and the hedonistic life-style—is just like placing a neon sign on the window of your temple.

The neon sign lets people know that things are for "sale here." It tells people what is inside. Your language tells people what is going on in your temple. It shows them what is going on upstairs in your mind and downstairs in your heart. Make no mistake about it: the things you say and do now as a young man will seem crazy when you have grey hair, and you watch young men say and do the same things.

The idea that there is something upstairs in your mind and downstairs in your heart is rooted in the fact of your body being a temple. Temples have an upstairs and downstairs. Both are deeply influenced by what you see and what you hear. Yes, that even means the fictional drama you watch on television, the music you listen to, and those video games! All you see and all you hear shape your beliefs. Your beliefs influence your language. And your language tells the world all about you. Good language is difficult to fake around people who are wise who speak it well. I pray that you are blessed with a life filled with people who are well-spoken and articulate but most importantly possess noble and godly character to back it up.

He who articulates well is able to advance further faster than a person who is not as articulate. To master your language requires an understanding of the language you speak, both verbal and nonverbal. Mastery of verbal language is to be able to use the right words in their proper usage, in the proper context, with the proper inflection. Mastery of nonverbal language includes reading their body language and requires you to understand all the contextual factors. The contextual factors are who you are talking to and what, when, where, and why you are talking to them.

It is extremely important that you learn this well, son: treat people with dignity and respect. How you treat others stems from your belief system and reflects who you really are. Your language must always be placed in the context of the belief that the person you are talking to is dignified and created by God. Even if they are evil heathens, speak to them with dignity and respect. I say this because there are too many "educated" people with lots of book smarts but no knowledge in how to treat others. C. S. Lewis said educated people with no morals are just more cunning devils. It is not good to master language and use it as a tool to abuse people or take advantage of them. If you treat them with dignity and respect because your beliefs are such that all men are created in the image of God, then you will be less prone to lie and manipulate for an upper hand. Mastering language is not meant for you to become manipulative. Remember, God sees and judges the motives of your heart. God is always watching.

Mastering language is not so that you can have the upper hand. It is certainly not for you to have ammunition to win arguments in order to feed your ego. Mastering language is good when it is aligned with speaking the truth, noble character, and bridge building. Use it to get yourself a place with the king of the palace and outside with the folks on the porch. Above all else, use it for good purposes. Good purposes are founded in love and compassion and concern for the well-being of others. Well-being is only well when it is righteous and just. It will likely take you many years to understand the true meaning of those two words.

Like all of the other tools, mastery takes practice and paying attention coupled to you actually knowing the words you are using. Knowing the words requires that you get an education. An education can be gained inside and outside of the classroom. Be careful to get both. Only learning inside the classroom is dangerous because formal education tells you what to think while informal education forces you to think for yourself. Both help you gain knowledge that is gainful if used correctly.

Take this analogy: A person is brought up in a palace. Every time they do anything, they are required to use the palace language and follow the palace rules. They talk stilted and mannerly. They sit at the table and eat stiffly. They ask to be excused from every social interaction. They are formal and proper. To you, they are over-the-top. They think that all social interactions are supposed to be like that; therefore, they seem awkward and unsociable when they are around the common folks outside the palace. Now imagine a person is brought up in a home that is more akin to a circus. Everybody is moving fast all the time (like most westernized homes). There seems to be no order to an outsider, but these people know the rules, and they move like a perfect storm. Dinner happens on the go. Their social etiquette is vastly different from the people in the palace. How could two people from these two very different backgrounds ever relate unless somebody is able to gain an understanding of the other's life? One is taught to be formal and the other informal.

The difference is like the difference of an education gained in the classroom and one gained outside of the classroom. One is formal, the other is informal. Both are useful. Both teach a different type of language and subjective perspective to go with it. You would probably be more likely to use the education you get inside the classroom less frequently unless you spend all your time in the classroom. Spending all your time in the classroom is no different than being confined in a building. People are meant to go outside. Freedom is always associated with the ability to go outside when you choose.

Confinement goes against all that I have written to you about. Your life is important, and liberty is best when you are free. Developing your language well helps you interact with all genres of people and age groups, thus enabling you fluidity of movement in any group wherever you may go.

The last thing an informal education gives you is the greatest variety of real-life scenarios to use in developing your language. It teaches you about the people. Everything in this world—the entire design of God's world—is for the people.

Love,
Dad

LETTER 9

Dear Son,

Boundaries are good, and boundaries are needed, but men do not want them. The antithesis between the two causes anxiety because men instinctively want to cross boundaries. We want to move as we choose. We men (and probably some women) want to come and go as we please. We are explorers, and we are curious. Curiosity is one of your tools. We want to wander and roam. We want to conquer. We do not want to be slowed down or hindered because of a boundary line. A boundary bounds you to a person, place, or ideology.

It is contrary to our nature because it is in our nature to move and be busy, even if that busyness is not actually doing anything significant. For example, you can be busy scrolling a Facebook profile. It is not in our nature to voluntarily choose to obey the boundaries without some sort of agreement. The agreement stems from moral laws and social rules. Both influence how a society writes its criminal laws and property regulations. It is dangerous when a society writes too many laws and regulations (boundaries) because the trade-off is liberty: just look at the amount of people with criminal convictions in America—a country that writes laws for everything yet claims to be the freest country in the world.

Being bound requires stillness. We humans dislike being still. Deep in the spirit, stillness is good. Stillness is necessary because it is during this time that growth happens. To be still means to be bound to a place. It is to be tethered. Unable to move freely. Some things need to be bound or life would be disorganized and chaotic. Your spirit is bound to your body. Your body is bound to the earth. Your mind is bound to your beliefs. Your mind is capable of pushing the boundaries as far as your imagination will let it. To be bound requires that you learn acceptance and patience. You learn acceptance and patience as you mature. Maturity is a sign of growing up.

You could be bound to anything. If your boundary is too small and narrow, then it will cause confinement. Confinement may cause mental health problems (a label that I absolutely abhor but use because modernity has made it a buzzword). If your boundary is too large and wide (liberal), then it will cause danger. Danger will cause physical and spiritual health problems. It is the principle of being bound that keeps your life structured and grounded. It shows the world that you are solid and committed, tied to something—God, family, friends, community, country, and world. Build your life in that order. That is the order beginning at that which is closest to you and working outward. Your connection to everything stems from your belief about those things.

Bound your beliefs to a right understanding of the Bible. A right understanding of the Bible does not twist the Bible to make it into a science book or expect it to tell you scientific things. Neither does it contort the Bible to make it say stuff that it does not. Nor is it supposed to be interpreted outside of the proper pretext and context. Set the foundation of your beliefs to the Bible. Wisdom will grow out of that. Wisdom will guide you to make good choices. Good choices are God-like, and they will help you have a good life by living in a God-like way.

Be bound to God and a proper view of God. You do not have the authority to judge people for God. Many people act like they do. They do not. There is only one moral lawgiver and one judge. That's God's job. Your job is to love Him and His creation. Do this, and peace is much easier to find. Joy is found with peace. A proper view of God is God as the creator, not the created. God is not in the earth or anything that a person on earth made. You cannot buy God. A proper view of God is God as the Savior. Think of the Savior as your lawyer. Remember, God gave the moral law, and all laws must be obeyed. You are bound to the law. You, like all of us, will break the law. In the end, God will judge according to the law. You need a lawyer. We'll call your lawyer Jesus. A proper view of God is that

His wrath should be feared, but His name and He Himself should be revered.

God loves you more than you can imagine. He loves you so much that He created the entire world for you. He made boundaries so that the world could spin and move a million miles a day and make a pattern of days and seasons so that those patterns could cause weather that sustains life, which leads to order that ultimately helps you make order in your own life. He did this all so that you could be a being. Humans give each other gifts which we make out of the stuff that God gave us on earth. Then we act as if we did that on our own. This is kind of like a child giving away his parents' stuff as a gift and forgetting that the stuff he gave away was not his in the first place. Small potatoes to God. God gave you the world out of His love for you. He set boundaries for the world so that it does not float off course in space, and then He bound you to the earth so that you do not float off into outer space. That's a pretty big deal!

To be bound means that you are shackled in some way. Be bound to God. Be bound to your beliefs about God. Be bound to your marriage. Stick with it. If it seems like it is failing, stick with it more. Try harder. Go the extra mile. Serve her like you want her to serve you. Love never fails. Love always prevails. Wisdom tells us that matters of love are bound by seasons. Fruit will appear if you are patient enough to let the winter season pass. The seasons are bound to their natural problems, which means that they must go through the full cycle to get back to the renewing season. Make boundaries that cover over your marriage. Boundaries are created as an agreement between people. Stay within the boundaries and order remains. Cross the boundaries and disorder happens. Boundaries are designed for safety, security, and peace, which makes prosperity on earth possible. To respect and obey the boundaries, you must learn to accept to be bound.

There is no such thing as absolute freedom on earth. Because you are capable of pushing past your natural physical limits by using your mind to create tools and technology, there must be a guide to keep you from using it to destroy yourself and others. Moral laws were written into the divine plan of your genetic code: the laws, boundaries, were written on your heart. You know what the bound-aries are. If there is a gray area between the culture you live in and you're understanding, then look to your Bible for clarity. Obey the boundaries, and your life will reflect your obedience. Be bound to those boundaries. They are intended so that you do not cross them and violate God—God's design and plan for you. The boundaries are also necessary so that others do not violate you or your property.

It is always best to manage your own property (affair) first before telling your neighbor how to manage his property (affair).

The Bible says, "Why do you look at the speck in your brother's eye, but fail to notice the beam [log] in your own eye?" (Matthew 7:3).

Think of a boundary as a lane when driving your car, if you choose to drive in the opposite lane, you are risking your life as well as those you may meet in their lane.

Follow God's leading; He will never mislead you.

Love,
Dad

LETTER 10

Dear Son,

Pride originates in man. Humility comes from the transformation of the heart when one accepts Jesus as Savior and Lord.

Pride is the original sin. God abhors pride. Pride happens when you forget that you were small once. Pride gets in the way in relationships. It gets in the way when it is time to apologize. It even gets in the way when it is time to forgive. Both are needed for peace after a war.

Pride comes from a place of desire and want. It is caused because you want people to believe a certain thing about you. It is the source of the superficial you—the reason you hide the skeletons in your closet and get so offended if they are brought out in to the open. It is the thing that keeps you from being real. Pride is the reason you put on the facade in public. It is the cause of your covering. It is a trait of Satan—the essence of who he is.

Do not confuse being prideful with being dignified. They are different. Pride is rooted in arrogance, and it influences how you act. Acting is a way of putting on, faking, or not being real. Acting requires a script. Dignity is rooted in nobility, and it influences how you view yourself and therefore how you carry yourself. Your nobility is established because you are a member of God's royal family. God is King of all. You are a member of His royal priesthood. You became a member when you accepted Christ as your Lord and Savior. Live your life like that is true! Be holy. Be gentle to the lowly and generous to the undeserving. No matter how much money is in your bank account, carry yourself like you have already been blessed with everything and share like the person you are sharing with is you.

Pride is a magnet. It leads you away from True North. It makes you forget where you came from and keeps you from going where you are supposed to go. It is a roadblock. Satan has figured out how to use it quite well. Pride is a thing that must be maintained. A person will abandon their morals to maintain their pride. They will ignore moral boundaries that they set for themselves and cross boundaries that others set too. Good men do not bend on their morals. Disciplined men obey the boundaries. Good men are obedient and disciplined. My prayer is for you to be a good man.

Pride gets in the way. It builds walls and tears down bridges. It ruins. It causes corruption. Corruption is what happens when purity is lost. Think of how fast metal is corrupted by rust once it is exposed. Your mind, your psyche, is as malleable and vulnerable as metal. Be careful what you open it up to. Do not be open-minded just because it sounds fashionable. Fashions change, and all is never fashionable. Corruption begins through the lust of the eyes and lust of the flesh. Satan used both to tempt Jesus. Satan knew what all good salesmen know: if he can just get his foot in the door, a foot-hold, then he can turn it into a stronghold because he can sow his seeds for a sale. If he can bend your mind to believe what he tells you because you "opened it up," you will renounce God for sin. Or you will ignore your boundaries. Sin is addictive. It yokes you to inevitable doom. Once you open your mind to sin, then you will likely choose sin because sin always seems safe in the beginning and then gets ignored when it becomes a habit until you believe that the sin is part of your identity. When you realize it is not, then you must admit your failure. Admitting failure is difficult because to admit failure is to renounce a part of the self that bought in to the lie that the sin was safe in the first place. Admitting sin takes humility from the sinner. When there is no light, a person only sees a pitfall once they are in the pit. Pride gets in the way of even seeing the pit. Pride is like cancer of the psyche. Pride requires a rehearsal.

Humility is the opposite of pride. It comes from a place deeper than the psyche. If your psyche is capable of expanding the boundaries of the imagination, the spirit is able to go through to the unimaginable. Humility is a kernel in the heart. Humility makes apologies and forgiveness easy. Humility is constructive. It is a foundational principle you must have in order for God's Word to make you into a righteous man. You cannot go before God without a humble heart. Humility is not to be confused with lack of self-esteem. Humility is to keep in mind that we all have thorns in the flesh. There are no perfect people. We all have our own problems and our own pain. We all have our own faults. Humility does not require a rehearsal. It is the belief that you do not need to fake who you are for others.

When you learn humility, you are being the most real version of yourself. The more humble you are, the easier it is for others to connect to you. Being humble allows others to be themselves around you. The ministry of Jesus Christ was so strong because he was able to get down to the bottom level with people because of His own humility. The only way God is able to get on man's level is by humility. There would be no Jesus if He was arrogant and pompous and prideful because people would be unable to connect. How easy is it to approach a person of high authority? Now imagine that person is also arrogant and prideful. They become unapproachable. The problem is that pride is a superficial characteristic, which is to say that it is fake.

How many babies do you know that worry about what others think of them? But the baby is the most attractive person in the room and the most honest at expressing themselves; why is that? It is Satan that wants you to believe that you need to be like that other person. All through your life, he will sow seeds of weeds that are intended to choke out the good seed that produces good fruit which gives you an abundant life. It is meant to draw your attention like a baby rattle does to a baby. If he can turn your attention away from the truth about what makes you rich, then he can slip in and steal your peace and joy.

And ultimately, peace and joy are the crown of life.

Love,
Dad

LETTER II

Dear Son,

The greater the calling on your life, the earlier on in your life that Satan will try to destroy you. You must always have your guard up, and you must always be aware of danger. Danger can come in the form of a magnet. Magnets keep you from finding your True North. Danger is in all things that God's Word commands you not to do. God's words are written in the Bible. There are commandments, and there are stories that show how disobeying those commandments cause danger. It is better to not get caught up on how disobedience causes danger, but rather, obey God's command because God said so. You do that because you love God.

Your dad on earth is much like our Father in heaven in the sense that he does not want to explain all the different reasons why you are not supposed to touch the hot stove. The reason is because I said so, but it is also because I love you, and I want you to keep from hurting yourself. That is the reason for God's Word, and that is the reason for these words. That is also the reason why the devil is determined to sow seeds of lies that dilute and pollute God's Word. Diluted words are not as meaningful. It is like having a rule that can be broken whenever it is convenient. That does not sound like much of a rule, does it? Do not believe the devil's lies. His goal is to destroy you and keep you from having an abundant life. Laws and rules are made for the disobedient, not for those sold out to Jesus.

Learn the Word so that you know the truth. When you know the truth, then you will understand why it was written in black and white. There is no gray area of truth. Truth by its nature is exclusive. The gray areas are subtle variations and half-truths, which is to say that they are not the truth. They are designed for trickery. They are intended so that you cross the boundaries under the wrong belief that the boundaries are there because our Father in heaven is just old-fashioned and mean and does not want you to have fun. That is ridiculous. God designed fun. The gray areas are meant to keep you from fulfilling the calling on your life. That is why the devil uses your youthful ignorance and emotions to lead you astray.

The devil will start on you while you are young. The wolf always goes for the baby sheep. It begins by separating the child from its mother. It uses chaos and fear to achieve its goal of killing the lamb. Unless you are a fully mature and stable Christian, then you are still a lamb. The devil will exploit your youth to lead you astray through ignorance. But you are not ignorant if you know the truth. You can only know the truth through study. Knowing the truth brings peace because it resolves questions of purpose and finality. Your life has meaning much deeper and wider than the meaning that society assigns it. Knowing the truth keeps you from being confused, which helps to keep your life in order.

Remember from a previous letter that you, as a whole person, are made up of three parts: spirit, mind, body. They are categorically different, but each deals with truth pertaining to its own category. There are spiritual truths that address things like love, peace, justice, righteousness, and wisdom. There are mental truths that stem from your beliefs and address how you interpret the world, your world-view. There are physical truths that address natural laws and the natural world, which you are able to interpret through your senses. If the devil leads you astray and your life is in chaos in any of these areas, to be the best version of yourself, take care to better yourself in all three parts of your being on a daily basis in this order: spirit, mind, body.

It is a mystery how God has braided them all together. You take care of yourself spiritually by following the laws of the spirit and through prayer and meditation and reading the Living Word daily. You take care of your mind through study, being creative, listening to pleasing sounds and music, seeing beauty, and good conversation. Good conversation is positive and stimulates your mind to think and be creative. It is not coarse language and talking about others. You take care of your physical part by eating healthy food that keeps your blood sugar moderate and by aerobic and anaerobic exercise.

Fasting helps all three parts. Go to bed hungry every night and fast from sundown to sundown for God once a week, and you will be well. Commit to this as an action of obedience to God. Learn these precepts early on in your life; obey them, and it will be well with you. The devil will have much trouble to destroy your life.

Love,
Dad

LETTER 12

Dear Son,

Sin and slavery go hand in hand. They are inseparable. Sin comes in three forms. You can sin in your heart; you can sin in your mind, and you can sin in your actions. The last two forms are taprooted in the first. They are born out of the heart. Slavery is addiction to anything you value more than God. How can you tell where your values are? Ask yourself what grabs your attention? What do you spend your money on? What do you spend your free time doing?

Unless you are illegally bound and your body is sold as a slave, then slavery happens first in the heart. Slavery to sin is rebellion against God. Jesus knew this. That is why he taught that adultery is not just a sin after it is acted out, but it is a sin once the thought is activated in the heart. The heart represents the spirit. Your spirit becomes a slave first. You (we humans) choose slavery. And you do not see the results until the consequences are evident in your life or until you are spending all your time, attention, and money on something that you are a slave to. My "persistent widow's prayer" for you is that you get wisdom early so that you do not spend the bulk of your life in slavery.

Slavery is a consequence of disobedience. To be disobedient is to rebel. Disobedience means to rebel against God's government. God's government has moral laws that are designed to keep order. We need order because people are dangerous. People are capable of destroying the entire earth and each other. Order is a necessary part for existence. When something is out of order, that means it does not work. Disorder in the human body is sickness. Disorder in the home leads to stress and struggle and discontent for the people that live there. Disorder on a job site causes confusion, slows work progress, and creates a dangerous environment. Disorder is when somebody is doing something they are not supposed to. Disorder in government causes the officials to worry more about power than the people. Disorder in society keeps people from living in peace and being prosperous. Disorder is contrary to God's design. God is God of order, not disorder. Disorder is a tool of the devil.

The outcome of willfully choosing to rebel against God is slavery. Slavery begins as a kernel in the heart. It blooms into a mindset. It creeps on like a growing waistline. It happens so gradually that you do not notice until the pants do not fit anymore. You are a slave if you are addicted to food or working out. You are a slave if you are addicted to sex, porn (sex with oneself), gambling, drugs, or alcohol. You are a slave if you are living in debt, but still want to shop using your credit card. You are a slave if you are unable to say no to that rebel, manipulative child. You are a slave if you think your stuff is more important than your salvation. You are a slave if Facebook, TikTok, or your phone is the first thing you look at in the morning.

You are getting it all wrong. You were not born with a slavery mindset. The belief that you need anything this world offers in order to have joy is a form of slavery. The devil needs slaves to build his kingdom. Jesus needs servants.

The bulk of the world is in slavery. Either they are slaves to their government, slaves to their work, or slaves to their stuff. They have willfully chosen this course. Many of the slaves are easy to spot. You may even see one in the mirror if you are honest. The slaves wake up and go to work to earn money that they have to give away the minute they get their paycheck. They hate work because they keep none of the money they earn. They are in debt for something that they were conditioned to believe that they need because a salesman told them so. Slavery is chosen by the self. In the same way that you have the right to choose your attitude in any given circumstance, you also have the right to choose liberty over slavery.

Liberty is freedom of the heart. If you want lasting change, start with the heart. But you must be honest to yourself about what you are enslaved to and what you need to change. Let go of that bitter experience that you are a slave too. Do not put on your boxing gloves to fight away the truth. Keep it real. Check your ego at the door. Your pride will only get in the way. Let go of it. Let go of all the stuff that is getting in the way. I am specifically not being specific so that you can assign these words to your own life. There is stuff that is getting in the way, and you know it. Your mind and spirit are unable to carry it. It weighs too much. Carrying too much weight for too long will wear you out. It is very difficult to win a war if you are worn out. The war is spiritual. The first form of slavery, slavery of the heart, is spiritual. Choosing slavery is a spiritual problem. It is personal.

The first commandment says, "You shall have no other gods before me." Placing anything in front of God is choosing slavery over liberty. The commandments are so that people can live in peace and gain prosperity. They are designed so all the people can be satisfied with life. God tells us to put Him first. If you place Him first, the natural outworking is that you will obey Him. Out of your obedience comes love, respect, gentleness, compassion, and care for everything on earth that God made, including yourself. Remember self is spirit, mind, and body. Giving you life is His greatest gift to you. Your greatest gift back is to love Him for the gift. In a sense, giving your life back in honor of Him. It works the best that way. Your life will satisfy you if you get this right.

May God always be with you, son.

Love,
Dad

Letter 13

Dear Son,

Take it slow and steady. Do not rush through your life and make yourself a slave from party to party, workday to workday, event to event. There will always be more parties, more work, and more events. One of the follies of youth is to think that you will miss something, to think you must be at every party and stay until the well is dry. Festivities and work are gifts, and gifts from God are good. Youthful energy and excitement about life is also a gift from God, but it has the best consequences if tempered by the boundary of responsibility. Responsibility comes from you honoring your commitments. The world needs more men to honor their commitments. Commitments and honor go hand in hand.

A commitment is something that you invest yourself in. It is an obligation that you willingly take responsibility for. Responsibility is to get more duties. You get more duties as you grow up. As you grow up, you gain more trust. As you gain more trust you learn to trust yourself. Your self-esteem increases. Responsibility is to take ownership of your life and the other stuff that is entrusted to you. It is to fulfill your duties. You will naturally hold your head higher as you live up to your responsibilities. Responsibility is learning to say no to the immediate gratification of a party and choosing to do the obligation you made early the following morning instead.

Growing up means you are responsible, and people can count on you. It means you are reliable. It is foundational to being a man. As you grow up, you will see more and gain more life experience. The more experience you gain, the harder it is to be impressed. It takes more to faze you. If you see too much too fast, you will become desensitized by life. This is what happens when you pack too many parties into your life. They all run together, and they lose excitement. They lose their thrill. The party becomes a habit rather than a celebration. You will become jaded. The downfall that goes with the pleasure-seeking lifestyle is expensive.

When you do anything too much, it forms a habit. The principle of habit forming applies to partying. It is like putting the same song on repeat and costing you money simultaneously. Some people dance to the same song through high school, some on into college, and some for their entire lives. Same song. On repeat. Sounds boring, right? It is. You can generally tell who spent the most nights partying by how they look when they are in their forties. Your body is meant to be cared for.

Too many parties mean you become a slave to the party while also giving up your responsibilities. You abandon maturity for a life of impurity. You become a slave to the belief that you will miss something if you do not show up. That is severely crippling logic because no person is able to go to all events all the time. How can you when you are only able to be at one place at a time? Only God is able to go to all things at once. All people miss all kinds of stuff, but they are not missing out by missing another thing. In other words, you miss every single party in this world that you are not at. You do not even know about the millions of parties going on, and you are just fine in spite of missing them. One more will not hurt you. That's rational. That is how mature adults think. The same people who are going to the party tonight will likely be at the next party next time.

Get it out of your mind to believe that you must make every party every time. It will turn into an expensive bad habit. Habits are very difficult to break because of the way that you are wired. After the habit forms, you consciously begin to identify yourself with that habit. If the habit is self-destructive, like too much partying, then you will lose yourself in the fog of the addiction while also seeing yourself as less.

You are not a drug addict. You are not an alcoholic. You are not a whore. Yes, men can be whores too. You are not a party animal. You are not a gossip hound. Can you see how all of those are indicative of a person having no self-control? One of the fruits of the spirit is self-control.

You were not meant to be shackled to any one of those things. If you choose that road, it will be a lonely road. Loneliness is bad for your health. It is dangerous. When a person is at the end of their life, the thing they want the most is not to be alone. Ironically, ignoring your responsibility will position you to be alone. To be alone is to be "all one." It implies without support and separated from others. It is different than learning to be autonomous as you grow up. Autonomy is to stand on your own. There is no implication that you lose support while learning autonomy. Standing alone is different from standing on your own, being autonomous.

Inherent in autonomy is responsibility. The important thing is to be responsible. Being responsible builds a framework for you to build your life. It pays off. Being responsible is to grow in your identity without burning bridges. If you burn too many bridges, then you ruin your own reputation and the ability to be trustworthy. Identity is how you view yourself. Reputation is how others view you. Be careful not to concern yourself with earning a reputation among the wrong people for the wrong reasons. Bad company corrupts good morals (1 Corinthians 15:33).

The wrong people are magnets, and they will keep you from finding your True North. You know they are the wrong people if they are caught up doing the wrong things.

     Read: self-destructive
     Read: lost with no direction
     Read: living for self
     Read: living with no plan for tomorrow
     Read: partying too much

My son, listen to my words. They come from experientially learned wisdom. They were bought with a heavy price. I spent forty years in the wilderness, running wild. My prayer for you is that you learn wisdom through my words. Use wisdom to make a safe boundary so that when your life is at the end, you can look back and know you fulfilled your purpose and you lived well.

Love,
Dad

Letter 14

Dear Son,

As you mature into a man, you must learn to take ownership of your stuff. To take ownership means you claim rights to something in your life. A thing may be a piece of property, a possession, your deeds or actions, a responsibility that you have been entrusted with, your words, your thoughts, and even the kernel of goodness or evil in your heart. To take ownership is to establish that it is yours. It takes a solid dude to shoulder the heavy weight of ownership over one's life.

When you shoulder the weight of something, you are doing more than claiming ownership. You are actually being the owner. You possess legal authority over it. It is rightfully yours. To be the owner means you bear the responsibility for it, which means that you get to enjoy the fruits or the misery that comes with owning it. If it is broken, fix it. If it was a bad plan that turned in to a failure, be honest and admit it. Take ownership for it. You cannot fix something if you act like it is not broken. If it was a stupid mistake, own it, correct it, make a better plan for next time, and move on.

When you take ownership, then you take possession of something. You claim authority over it and you claim responsibility for it. It takes large character for you to do this because some of your stuff is unattractive. Some is downright embarrassing. Do you blame others for a failure? Do you judge people that are different than you? Do you gossip? Do you speak bad about a person behind their back? Do you think you are more deserving of God's grace than the next man? Do you glance over that attractive lady with a ring on her finger? Do your eyes go to her chest when she walks up and her rear when she passes? Do you get out the porn when nobody is home? Do you offer to buy dinner, but when the bill shows up, you silently regret being kind? Would you say what you were thinking at the time you had that mean thought to the person you thought it about?

The common denominator for all of these is that they are done in secret. The secret may be yours. God knows you own it. But do you *own* it? As in, are you willing to take responsibility for it if it is a complete and utter failure? How about if you can get away with blaming another person? Do you own it if your secret becomes public? It takes much humility to say you have done something wrong. But it is a much heavier load to carry a secret than to release it and say you have done something wrong. Humility is the key ingredient to be a righteous man. To be a righteous man is to be on the right side of God. You are righteous when you have right morals, and you make wise decisions based on right morals. You are also righteous when you are faithful to God.

Faith in God is born out of fear of God. Fear of God comes from knowing how small you are to God. Fear of God is when you are wise enough to know that God has given the moral law, and at the end of your life, you will be made to give an account of all the laws you broke in your actions and your heart; judging the heart is about intention. Fear of God is to know that you will take ownership of your secrets when you have to go in front of God. Fear of God causes you to live your life in accord with his moral law. The principle can be shown with this analogy: fear of fire causes you to keep from sticking your hand in the fire. You do not test the fire. There is a penalty if you test the fire and do not obey your fear. In the same way that you would keep your physical body out of the fire because of fear, you must protect your spiritual body from the fire of judgment, which is a lake of fire we call hell. You will be required to take ownership of all that you did or did not do in your life.

Learning the principle of ownership now will help you live a good life. It will guide you to stay in the boundaries and keep you humble enough to admit when you cross them. It is necessary for self-correction.

As you mature into a man, take ownership of your life. Even the details matter. You cannot do this on your own strength. You must put your faith in Jesus who will give you the strength you need when you need it. Have discipline in the small stuff, take ownership, and your mindset will carry over to the big stuff. Be responsible of all that you are given charge of, and you will be given more. Be humble and honest enough to admit a fail. It is okay! Every person is responsible for countless fails. Stay clear of those who believe they have never failed. They are easy to spot. When disaster strikes, they are the ones who are unwilling to accept responsibility. They blame everybody but themselves. They only take ownership when it makes them look good. That is called shallow. Shallow is a description of how deep a thing may go. It has nothing to do with the outside parts that we can see like their looks, possessions, job title, or place in society. It has everything to do with their depth of character, which is the part that we can't see. Character is who they are when nobody else is looking.

Real people have real problems, and they are real far from perfect.

You are one step closer to the best version of yourself if you are humble enough to take ownership of your problems and imperfections. When you own them, you are actually shining a light on them; that way, you are able to fix them. You were born capable. A pillar of your foundation growing up is learning what you are capable of then stretching your capabilities to get the most out of yourself: to don your cape because of your abilities.

To say it another way, growth is enabled by taking ownership of all the things that you have which affect your life so that you can live your best life.

Love,
Dad

LETTER 15

Dear Son,

Taking ownership requires a combination of humility and strength. Strength is an element of character that loses its virtue if humility is missing. Humility will keep you on the right side of God. Humility is when you have the courage to say you made a mistake openly, and repent. Humility necessitates honesty. It requires for you to give an honest assessment of self. It is better to learn humility by listening to wisdom than by learning through failure. Listen to me and learn from me. Pray for discernment and wisdom which Jesus will give freely to those who ask.

Failure is expensive. The cost multiplies if you are unable to admit the truth about why you failed or why something you have done did not work. The longer a failure is left unchecked, the more costly and the more difficult it is to get yourself back on track. If it goes on too long, you will need a supernatural intervention to fix it. Some people call that a miracle.

Humility does not mean lack of confidence. Humility is to be confident enough. It means you are secure enough with yourself not to place your ego ahead of wisdom and righteousness. Righteousness is to know the morally right thing to do. Wisdom is what causes you to choose the right thing to do. To choose to do the wrong thing is to act foolishly. You were not born a fool. You learn to be a fool by listening to other fools. This is why there are so many fools in the world.

Sometimes, doing the right thing will be very hard because humans are naturally inclined to take the easy way. One of the goals of these letters is to teach you not to take the easy way just because it seems easy at first. Just because it is easy does not make it right. Oftentimes, the easy way is not the right way. The easy way should not be confused with the simple way. The easy way is deceptive in the beginning because of its ease, but it may cause hardship and difficulty later, like telling a little white lie to detour confrontation or lying to make yourself appear better. That is called being fake or deceitful.

Simple means uncomplicated. Simple means clear. Clear is transparent. It is simple to take ownership if you are humble because win or lose, right or wrong, your ego is not as important as the higher principle of righteousness. It becomes much more complicated and unclear when you try to preserve your ego. You will know that you are preserving your ego because you will be less transparent. Be careful to not let your ego get in the way of any aspect of your decision-making process. Your ego is the root of choosing to do something for the wrong reasons. Put simply, your ego will cause you to do something stupid for the wrong reason.

This does not mean to not take pride in your work nor does it mean not to work harder to improve. That is different than ego. That is called self-respect, which is respecting yourself enough to care about being better. God wants you to be the best version of yourself, but it must not come at the cost of doing the wrong thing for the wrong reason. Do not make that trade.

The key to it all is to check the motivation behind what you do. Ask yourself why you are really doing something. Did I do this kind act because people are watching? Did I do it because I think God will repay me later? Or did I do it because I love God and love the people He created? Ultimately, it boils down to where your heart is at. If you love God and have a heart for God, then you will love His creation and act accordingly.

When two people are in a relationship, that relationship develops around their common interests and grows into their interests in each other. Love blooms out of that. Love, like all the other virtues, is for interpersonal relationships. Contrary to what the culture says, love is not a term that is meant to be used for stuff. In the same vein, other virtues like justice and righteousness are not to be used for your stuff. By using the term love to describe a relationship to your stuff, it shades the meaning of the term thus making it watered-down. It makes it less clear.

Love and repentance is what your relationship to God is founded on. It is the foundation of it all. It is the kernel for the connection. And, like all your other relationships, it influences how you see the world and how you act in the world and you respond toward the world or how you connect to the world. How many people do you know that are genuinely in love and you can tell even when they are not with their lover? Their world is brighter. You can read it on their face. They exude the joy of loving somebody and being in love deep in their soul. They are brighter, more confident, and generally more optimistic about life. Ask yourself how they act when they are fighting with that same lover? Now ask yourself how they are when they do not have love at all? Can you imagine a world where love is completely missing? God is love, so a world with no love would be a world with no God. Depressing huh?

When a person is in a relationship to God, similar inter-relational dynamics are at play. They share the same interests as God, His kingdom, and His business. They share that relationship with others. They talk to Him often which does not only consist of asking for favors. Can you imagine a relationship with somebody where the person only talks to you when they want something from you? It does not feel like love. It is one-sided and unbalanced.

A loving relationship is when two people are able to be themselves. They are able to give and receive. It is humble and simple. They are able to be transparent. It is not complicated. It does not change when one person is unable or unwilling to do every single thing the other person asks. In a loving relationship, the person asking says, "I'll do it myself, and while I'm at it, I will do something for you too."

A good relationship brings light into both lives. It glorifies both people. A good relationship takes two people that are willing to take ownership for their role. Learn to take ownership early. If not, you are simply putting off the inevitable. The inevitable is that the truth always comes to light and if you have neglected to take ownership this time, you may have to deal with it next time or you may create a dangerous habit of neglecting what is important in your life. Nothing can create more pressure on you than putting the important stuff off. When you start down this path, you are going the wrong way, and you will end up in the wrong place.

Having a relationship with God is the most important thing you can do in your life. Make it early. And it will bring fruit long after you are gone. The Hound of Heaven, as C. S. Lewis calls the Holy Spirit, enters your heart when you accept Jesus to make sure you make it to heaven. Your responsibility is to listen to Him and let Him guide you on all you do.

Love,
Dad

LETTER 16

Dear Son,

A sign for everybody that you are growing up is that you will be stable. Mental, emotional, and spiritual stability will lead to financial stability. Financial stability is valuable, but we will focus on the mental, emotional, and spiritual. The backbone of stability in your life is your relationship to God. He is the Grand Weaver that weaves all the threads into a beautiful tapestry so that you have an individualized story of your life. The hard, difficult, and coarse threads (the trials and tribulations of your life) are the threads that make your tapestry strong, durable, and resilient. They are as necessary to your life story as words are to a book.

They are intrinsic qualities of you. They are within you! You were born with them! You may not realize it, but they are there! Oftentimes, it takes a difficult circumstance to pull those qualities out of you. Stability is a learned quality. Stability means steadiness, balance, and dependability. It is a trait of a mature man. It is a trait that is naturally groomed as you grow in wisdom. It is a trait that brings fruit.

Stability. Stay-ability. It is rooted in your contentedness.

It is your ability to stay the course. It is what causes you to make adjustments when things are not going as planned, to self-correct. A characteristic of stability is that there is an end goal. There is movement toward that goal. You are guided by a purpose. But this does not mean that you are not always stationary. Sometimes the goal is to be there for somebody during a difficult period, which requires you to settle and be still. Goals are a necessary element of maturity.

One of the few things that Freud says that I actually agree with is, "Maturity is your ability to postpone gratification."

Learning to wait is essential to personal growth and maturity. From the beginning to the end, your life is on a trajectory that develops and changes and grows with your body, time, and life experiences. You are constantly changing with time in your body which corresponds with your life experience which ultimately causes you to see the world differently. God is outside of all that. God does not change. God remains the same. When God sees the world, He sees the entire picture. Seeking God is where you will find your true riches because God shines light on the riches you already have. You will see the world as God does. God will guide you to your True North. True North is to follow the way of your purpose. How could anything except that which never changes guide you to your True North? True North is a specific direction. What would happen if the North Pole always changed its position? Your GPS would be useless because every longitudinal and latitudinal point would be thrown off.

You would get lost.

Faith in God is when you trust God to guide you to your True North. Faith in God is to know that even when you are unable to see how things are going to turn out, you believe that you are still not lost, and you are on the right track. Faith is when you are able to perceive and move forward without physically seeing or hearing. Reason supports your ability to perceive. To perceive is to have knowledge and understanding with both the mind and the heart. Reason happens in the mind. Faith happens in the heart. You were born with both. Just like you were born with muscles, but they only develop with use. So too faith and reason only develop with use. You must pay close attention so that you get knowledge and understanding with both. Knowledge and understanding will help you see the world like God does. Knowledge and understanding will keep you from wrong thinking which lead to bad choices.

Bad choices are the signature of an unstable man.

Can you imagine if a blind man was taken into a monastery filled with monks who had made a vow of silence? Would he know they were there? Yes, because there would be several clues like the fact that somebody would have led him there. But there would be other clues like the fact that there is a building in the middle of nowhere, and everything has a place, and the place itself has the smell of people. He is probably even able to detect the aura of them. What is aura but energy through warmth.

His reasoning allows him not to see the people every day yet to know that they are still there. His faith allows him to trust that even if he could no longer detect any clues of the humans, he will make his life based on the belief that they are still there. Reason is for the here and now. Faith is for the future.

Faith is fundamentally different than reason. Faith is stronger and deeper. Where reason is drawn from information outside of you, faith is drawn from within. Faith will stabilize your life. It is easier to be around a stable person, and it is better to be in a relationship with a stable person than an unstable person. People are able to count on you if you are stable.

Social status is not something I want you to worry about, but a natural by-product of your stability is that it improves your social status. With a higher social status comes more resources to help bring others up. To bring others up is foundational to fulfilling your purpose. It is a form of ministry simply called loving your brother.

Stability is your ability to be bound to a specific goal and purpose. It requires you to be disciplined and intentional. It tells people that you have thought this through, and you are committed; you are staying.

Not all people are stable. Many are unstable and therefore many are lost.

If you want to get the most out of your life, you must learn stability. You must practice stability. You must take it slow and steady. Be stable. Even the ant is stable because it is able to stay the course because it knows its purpose, and because it knows its purpose, it is never lost.

Love,
Dad

Letter 17

Dear Son,

The diamond only becomes a diamond with lots of heat and pressure. A lump of coal must endure heat and the pressure long enough so that the substance of what it is changes. It takes heat and pressure for the entire chemical structure to recombine. It reforms into something harder, long-lasting, and more durable. The heat and pressure transform a common mineral into a precious, rare jewel. But it takes years of endurance before it makes the transformation from common to rare.

Besides taking part in making a baby, no valuable thing is easy to make. Oftentimes, the more difficult something is to make, the more valuable it is. Value also goes up when more time is spent on making something. This is why a marriage increases in value the more time you spend in your relationship with your wife. The inverse of this principle is that it also costs more if you choose divorce. The principle that value goes up with "time and energy spent" is basic to the economics of relationships. It is why raising a boy into a man is so difficult and important and simultaneously valuable.

Men bear the responsibility for the family, the community, and the nation. A strong nation needs men of work, men of war, and men of prayer. America was at her most prosperous, strongest, and safest when this pattern was followed. It was also the freest with the least amount of laws and the lowest corresponding prison population. The same pattern can be collapsed so that a community needs men of prayer, men of work, and men of war (men willing to fight for righteous moral reasons). Even further, every dad needs to be a bit of all three.

When dad is missing, everything possible is wrong. Think about the disasters for a nation when there is no moral leadership (men of prayer), no military (men of war), and no men willing to work. The people would be at the behest of whatever the powerful person who takes interest in them chooses. Most likely, they would be slaves and starve! History is replete with examples of this happening. You can fit the story of a family into the same paradigm: the dad who is not a man of prayer, the dad who is not a man willing to work, or the dad that is not willing to fight for the moral uprightness of his family and see why there are so many social issues today.

We live in a country with the "absent dad" problem. It is like cancer. Cancer is when a cell teaches other cells to do the wrong thing, thus ruining the entire body. The absent dad problem means that dad is unable (incarcerated or blocked by mom), unwilling (leaving the kids with a caretaker all day), or incapable (dad was taught wrong) of teaching his son how to be a man. Put another way, dad teaches his son to do the wrong thing thus multiplying the effect out into the community. One dad teaches his two children, two children teach their four children, four children teach their eight children, the children go to school and influence each other and so on.

For the family to thrive, the man must intentionally fulfill all of those roles. If you want to create the best environment possible for your own children to be prosperous, strong, and safe, then stick to this pattern: be a man of prayer, a man of work, and a man of war. The families, communities, and nations that follow this pattern are always most successful. Just look at the neighborhoods where the people have the nicest houses, best jobs, best health, best education, and live the longest, all of which get passed on to their children. The common denominator is that those neighborhoods are filled with complete families, where this pattern is being followed. Church attendance is high, unemployment rate is low, and they do not tolerate crime.

You cannot make a change in the nation without starting with the family. And you cannot be a man that your kids call dad without going through the heat and pressure that comes with that role. Absent dad means that there is no man to teach the boy (child) to be a man that has the humility to pray, the fortitude to work hard for what he wants, and the will to fight for the right things. Out of that is an ingredient to fulfilling your purpose, and ultimately, true riches are found in that.

Being a human is tough. It is filled with struggle, pressure, and pain. Being a dad is also filled with struggle, pressure, and pain. In fact, struggle, pressure, and pain are multiplied the more children a dad has because he bears the weight with each individual child.

Struggle, pressure, and pain are a necessary part of the transformation process so that true riches are found. It is like going through an education of hard knocks so that you understand in your soul, body, and spirit what those riches are. Think about it. Jesus was the one person in the world who could choose His own fate, and He chose pain. He chose pain because pain is a fundamental thread of humanity. Pain sucks, but so does the five-o'clock workout. Hidden inside the workout are countless benefits, especially health. Struggle, pressure, and pain are like a workout for the spirit. They are intended to make you better by stretching you and causing you to expand.

Even a cake must go in the fire before it expands and rises.

Your life is important. Your life has value. Do not waste it. There will be triumphs, and there will be pain. Pain helps you find purpose. It makes meaning personal. It teaches you what true riches are. A person is generally unaware about the value of their health until they have a close call with cancer. People get much more reflective about life when a young person dies. And they learn to appreciate their life when parts of it are lost.

Pain makes life personal. It is a necessary thread so that you can become the best version of yourself. There are no champions that have not been through it. And there are no men that must not eventually go to battle and conquer it.

Love,
Dad

LETTER 18

Dear Son,

Be teachable. You do not know it all nor do you understand everybody's point of view. Do not argue your side without knowing the other side. To know is to have intimate understanding of. You will save yourself a lot of headaches, heartaches, and maybe even a heartbreak if you remain silent when you do not know the other side. A folly of the youthful, arrogant, ignorant, and proud is to pretend like one is more knowledgeable than one is. It is an unattractive quality for you to avoid.

Keep your mouth shut and keep yourself from being a fool.

Being teachable requires you to be humble enough to admit that you do not know something. The first step to attaining wisdom is the fear of the Lord. The second step is to be teachable. All people who know it all do not need to be taught. Nobody knows it all. Therefore, all people need to be taught. That is a basic syllogism. A syllogism is a form of a logical argument. It is a statement that does not contradict itself—a truth statement.

Willingness to be teachable is an attractive trait. It is important so that you are able to grow as a man. There are way too many know-it-alls that know very little. The world does not need another one. To be teachable is a natural by-product of humility. Humility is to remember that you were like a child once. Which age group is the easiest to teach? Children! With humility, you are showing a willingness to listen and follow instructions.

Teachability is a growth mindset. It is a mind set for growth. There is no fruit until something grows. It is very simple. Remember, simple is clear. Clear is the opposite of confusing. Confusion is disorder. If God's kingdom is His domain and He is a God of order, then disorder is the devil's domain. To be teachable does not only mean that you have eyes to see but ears also to listen and hands to work. It means that you are also willing to follow instructions properly, which is to obey.

Be careful to only follow good instructions. You must use discernment so that you do not follow stupid instructions. Also, do not challenge everything because you think it is stupid. The dictionary does not define stupid as "something you do not want to do or do not agree with." Stupid, by definition, is unintelligent, dazed, and unable to think clearly.

It is direly important that you know right from wrong because if you are taught the wrong thing and follow that route, it will have disastrous consequences in your life. Furthermore, when you act something out, others see and learn from you. It may be a good thing or a bad thing that you teach them. If it is bad thing, this will have disastrous consequences for you and the entire community. I knew a man that showed a boy how to steal, and when the boy grew up, he robbed the man and stole his life. Teaching boys the wrong thing will crumble any society. The wrong thing could be anything that is not, first and foremost, morally upright.

Do not allow yourself to get trapped in the weeds of "gray area" and "what if" moral scenarios.

The first and most important thing to learn is to fear God. Fearing God is the foundation to attaining wisdom, and it is also the anchor of righteousness. What is righteousness but upright moral behavior. It is the exact opposite of wickedness. It is the most important part of the equation for living a good and solid, purpose-driven life. Righteousness is counted as faith. And faith helps you get into heaven. It looks forward. To be teachable is a childlike trait. Jesus says, "For the kingdom of Heaven belongs to such as these."

Be teachable.

Ignorance is the hallmark of a person who has not been taught. It is an unattractive, anthemic quality. It keeps you from rising up to be the best version of yourself. You will not find true riches if you choose to follow the path of ignorance. How could it when your ignorance does not allow you to search for what true riches even are? In other words, how would you know you found something if you don't know what you are even looking for?

You will normally find like minds around each other—those that are ignorant and those that are hungry to be taught. Ignorance is the cornerstone of a man that has a lot to complain about. He has no plans nor does he have plans to improve his lot. He is easy to spot; he is the one that blames everybody but himself. Avoid him at all costs. You have no business trying to rescue a drowning swimmer when you barely know how to swim yourself.

The synergistic principle works for ignorant people too. Like minds group together, and ignorance is multiplied by the nature of grouped energy. Think of it as being among all those drowning people on the Titanic—flailing arms and panic. The impending doom is inevitable. Now imagine that none of them can swim.

To be teachable means that you are malleable, bendable, and able to receive knowledge. It is the catalyst that makes you able to grow fruit out of the riches that you were born with. Think of it like fertilizer for the fruit. It is great gain for you to be teachable.

As you go out in the world and learn more, always know that good and evil are real. Even the atheist believes in evil when it is done against them. You were taught the difference between good and evil. Always weigh your choices through the lens of good and evil. Learn the simple version (the Ten Commandments) and stick to it. The devil will attempt to deceive you. Stay away from evil people, evil actions, and evil ideas. Evil is infectious. It is the easy way. It can be taught. Remember you learn through the eyes and ears. The seeds of evil must enter through there. Bad company corrupts good morals (1 Corinthians 15:33).

As you mature into a man, it becomes your personal responsibility to teach others that which is good while standing up against that which is bad. It is the proper way for a society to pass goodness on or the society crumbles. The societies that teach evil and promote unrestricted hedonism do not make it. Take a look at every nation throughout history. There is only one that has survived the longest and remain relevantly prosperous: Israel. It is the one society that stuck to the principles of righteousness that the Bible teaches—the same principles that I am trying to teach you through these letters.

Learn as much as you can along the way because it will make a difference throughout your entire life. It will get you much further while also leaving your own children in a much better spot.

Love,
Dad

LETTER 19

Dear Son,

If you want something, do not just wish for it; work for it and save for it.

Be persistent. Work hard. Save.

Persistence is a trait you were born with but must learn to apply in order to be effective. It is about movement toward a goal. It is a forward-looking trait—the outworking of faith. To be persistent is to be determined and unrelenting. It is an action-packed word. It is not to quit once you commit to a goal. Goals are very important, and so is achieving them. They are important for you to gain a good self-image and healthy self-esteem. Both of which help you stand up taller and attempt more stuff.

To many failed attempts when you are pursuing your goals can be destructive if you do not harness the trait of persistence that you were born with. So that you don't "fail," set your long-term goals in increments. Break them down into steps. Each step gets you closer to your goal. Even if the step is a step that simply reroutes you toward the goal, keep your focus, learn from the failure, adjust, and lean in. Go for it again.

Just remember that it took Edison over a thousand attempts to make the light bulb. To be a master at something, you must work at it for roughly ten thousand hours. That's full time, forty hours a week, for five years. If you play your cards right, you can master three or four different things over the course of your life. Remember, mastery applies to doing things that are harmful too like lying, stealing, and cheating. Of course, the results will be obvious depending on what you choose to master.

Make sure that you do not set your goals too low. Expect a lot out yourself. Understand that if the goal is set higher, then it will take more time and more effort to achieve the goal. More energy will be necessary to achieve a higher goal. It takes much more fuel to fly to the moon than it does to fly across the state. Not surprisingly, there are a lot less people that get to the moon, and the view is much better.

The key is to maintain dogged determination. Do not be distracted. Do not take your eyes off the goal. Do not give one thought to the energy that has already been spent out or how worn out you are. Those are mere distractions. Focusing on those will slow you down from getting to your goal. Focusing too long will completely sidetrack you. It is a distraction.

Dis-traction means to lose tracking. To lose your tracking is to slip. It is to go out of balance, which means you are likely going down. Dis-traction causes you to be side-tracked.

Beware of getting side-tracked.

There is not a more common shared trait among men than how easily distracted we are. Distraction will keep you from being the best version of yourself. It makes for a lot of unfinished projects in the garage. It also makes for lots of unfinished New Year's resolutions. You want to know the external ability of yourself? Just look at the number of projects you are able to think up, start, and finish on your own. Notice that I did not say "projects you direct others to finish for you." That does not count here, and that is not what I am talking about. A rich guy can pay to get his projects finished. Money can make it easier to get things done. You can pay somebody to complete a project for you. But I am not talking about that or the person who you paid to do that for you. I am talking about the projects you start and finish on your own, the projects that you take complete ownership of by doing yourself. That is the measuring tape for how well you follow through, not the guy that you hired.

These letters are not for him. They are for you. I want you to be the best man you are capable of being. There is a lot more to being a man than getting taller and growing muscles. Being a man implies having certain intrinsic qualities like having the ability to plan, start, and finish a project. It is to take ownership of your own stuff and to make the most of what you have.

In general, I am talking about you, your relationships, and your castle—the blessings that God has placed in your domain.

Persistence. Persistence is a steady movement toward a goal. Persistence is chain linked to commitment and focus. Commitment is the driving force, and focus is the guiding force. Persistence is a force of the will. Force is invisible energy. Even the scientist has difficulty explaining the concept of force as it pertains to his own senses of interpretation of reality. He can use math to quantify and make a prediction, but he can't smell, taste, touch, hear, or see it. He simply and intuitively has faith that it is there. Oddly, he makes fun of the Christians for believing in a God that we can't smell, taste, touch, hear, or see while ignoring this fact upon which his entire system of science is built upon: the four forces.

Persistence is a building block that you need so that you can get the most out of your frontal lobe, the planning part of your brain. It is a tool that you were born with. A construction worker is unable to make something until he gets his tools out and uses them.

You must learn to use your tools to get the most out of them. You can only really learn them by rolling your sleeves up and getting your hands dirty. Getting in the mud and trying life. Going after life.

Fail?

Try again. Keep trying. Be persistent. Eventually, you will get it right, and you will have gained immensely. Your gain will be through your experience in tough times, which is arguably the best kind. Trial by fire leads to experience, and experience gains wisdom. It is another piece of the puzzle which ultimately helps you for the bigger picture: to be the most you can be by developing the tools you were born with.

Surprisingly, every person is born with the same tools. They only show up when they are used. Some people use their tools so often they seem better equipped and more rounded. You can too if you learn to use your own tools and do not try for the easy way in your life.

Persistence is when you continue to use your hammer despite smashing your thumb after the first try. You were born with it! That is why the three-year-old will ask for something until he gets it. The trait in and of itself is good, but it is only good if it is guided by goodness.

Persistence to the positive. Sometimes, the thing that yields the most positive results is the thing that is hardest for you. If the three-year-old gets his way every time, then he'd be a spoiled brat, maybe ruined. Train your persistence toward that which is good for you—God, family, positive relationships, a healthy lifestyle, learning, and making something, then your life will go well.

Love,
Dad

LETTER 20

Dear Son,

Work hard.

Be disciplined.

Save your money.

Do not ignore this letter or write it off as unimportant, cliché talk. If you do, I promise you will regret it when you need it most.

Do not be the guy that works all week to turn your entire paycheck over. If so, you are merely a slave to the debtor, a slave to the bills. If you are working just to pay the bills, then you need to make lifestyle adjustments so that you are able to save a percentage of your paycheck every time. Learning to be disciplined in this area of your life is the only way that you will get ahead and be ahead in the later years of your life. Saving money gives you more options when you need them. Freedom is to have more options.

Saving is a lifetime discipline. Discipline is fortitude, commitment, and self-control. It is the thing in your life you can choose to have control over. No matter the circumstances, you have total control over the amount of discipline you have in your life—when you wake up and go to bed, what you do with your time, how well you take care of yourself and your stuff, how much effort you put into your work, and the amount of money you save are all a reflection of your self-discipline.

A reflection is when a life picture is thrown back at you. It is very important that you see a truthful reflection as it is without any distortions. Distortions happen when pride and ego get in the way and cause you to make excuses and lie to yourself about the problem rather than fix it. A distortion is a misrepresentation that causes a misinterpretation. It will keep you from an honest evaluation of yourself.

Discipline is attached to a goal. Discipline is action-oriented toward a goal. Merely thinking about something does not mean that you have discipline. You can make all the resolutions you want, and they are no good as long as you do not put them into action consistently for the long term. Discipline is a resolution with commitment.

In order for you to achieve a goal, you must make incremental steps toward the goal. A goal keeps you on track. It gives you something to focus your energy on. Focus keeps you from wandering. Focus and energy and discipline are tools in your toolbox. You were born with all of them. Like your muscles, you must use them to get strength and muscle memory. If you practice discipline, it will become a part of who you are. It will be how you are defined. Discipline is the tool you will need to get up, go to work, and then save a portion of your paycheck. It is what keeps you from staying out late when you know you have to work early. It is what keeps you from pulling out a credit card when there is no money in the bank account. It is what causes you to push yourself away from the table rather than overeat. Discipline is to make the right choice when presented with a chance to make the wrong choice.

To save is to put something away for the future. It is an action verb. It is to stow away. It is simply a word until you put it in to action. Your words gain power when you are a man of action. Until you put them to action, they are merely empty and no more dangerous or powerful than a written word in a dictionary.

There are three kinds of people: those that plan for the future and do something about it, those that plan for the future and do nothing about it, and those that have no plans at all.

The first kind are rare. They are the ones that leave their children the most inheritance. They work and save most of their lives. They have confidence in themselves because they have followed through on their dreams. They are established because they have chosen to be disciplined. They will leave a will for their children because they planned for it their entire lives. They have others working for them to make their dreams come true.

The second kind are the most abundant. They are the dreamers. What is a dream but a thought that happens in an unconscious state, outside of reality. For the majority of the people in this world, dreams never become a reality because they are never put into action. It remains in the "thought" stage. It simply dies with the person. It is for this reason that the graveyard may be the richest place in the world. The dreamer never rises to their full potential. This is the group that gets up and go to work to make another person's dream come true.

The last kind is in self-destruct mode. They are satisfied being lost. They don't have foresight. They have short sight. They are stuck in the here and now, and so they do not use the frontal lobe, which is the biggest part of the brain. Your brain is the gift that will get you the furthest ahead in your life. The last kind of people are the ones that make the bulk of their decisions trying to satisfy the reptilian brain. The reptilian brain is the part of the brain that deals with food, sex, fear, and pleasure. It is also called the pleasure center of the brain. These are the ones that waste their lives. Can you imagine living a life where eating, sex, and partying are the sole motivation? It would be a disaster. Look at Solomon.

You would be a slave to your body, and you would never be satisfied. Discipline is the action of committing yourself to something faithfully. Learn to have discipline over your wallet. If not, you may as well let the corporation have their hand in your wallet.

Work hard and save your money. If so, you will be prepared when an emergency happens. The more money you save, the more opportunities you create. Money in the bank makes you able to be a part of a money-making opportunity when it happens. That's how people get ahead. You have heard the old saying, it takes money to make money, right? Meaning, you will need money for the initial startup.

Save for seed money.

Save for safety net money.

Safety net money will only be there if you put it there and let it pile up without spending it as soon as you get it. Having it there will leave you in a much better position in life. Positioning is key to social success. Good positioning only happens by being at the right place at the right time. Being at the right place only happens by doing the right thing. The right thing is that which is righteous. Saving is a Biblical principle, which makes it a righteous principle. So is giving back a portion of what you make.

If you fail here, you are going in the wrong direction, and you will end up in the wrong place in your life.

Love,
Dad

LETTER 21

Dear Son,

Show me your friends, and I will show you your future. Choosing good friends is very important. Every choice that you make in your life will have consequences. Some are positive, and some are negative. Some will make you feel good, and others will make you feel bad. The greater the decision, good or bad, the greater the consequence and the greater the need for wisdom when making that decision—the more thought you need to put in to making that decision. Who you choose to be friends with will have greater consequences that impact your life than nearly every choice you make.

People are easy to influence. If the same message is repeated enough, eventually, you will believe it. That is why it is so important that you guard your ears diligently. If you hear something enough, you will believe it. The people you are around the most are who speak the most to you, and they, in turn, influence you the most. If merely being around a person has the power to influence you, then it is wise to use caution about who you allow to be around because you are giving them power over your life. You are giving them power to influence what you like, how you act, how you dress, how you talk, and, ultimately, what you believe about the world, all of which have great ramifications for you.

What you believe determines how you respond to the world and, in turn, how the world responds back to you. It is based on the rule of reciprocity. If you act like a fool, the world will treat you like one. If you fake like you are not but do things that suggest that you are, then you will get found out because the truth always comes to light. No fool can fake it for too long. Remember these two basic social rules:

1. You will be treated based on how you act.
2. You will act like the people around you.

Those are basic social rules, and if you choose poorly, the consequences will be very, very costly. Even so, you are responsible for your own choices. You will be held accountable for your *own* choices. Everybody has to pay the piper. Grown-up choices cost grown-up prices. At the end of the day, you cannot blame your outcomes on your friends. As you make your way up higher on the ladder in your various roles in society, you will be given more responsibilities that require more accountability. You will have to give an account to somebody. Responsibility is for you. Accountability is for others. Blaming a friend for bad choices that you made is not acceptable. What would you think if somebody violated you and then said, "But don't blame me; blame my friend."

Ted Haggard said, "Sin will take you farther than you want to go. It will keep you longer than you want to stay, and it will cost you more than you want to pay."

Choose your friends well, and when things go bad, you will have a person to lean on. It is a good thing for your spirit to have a solid friend in your corner. There are plenty of studies that show people who have lifetime friends live longer lives. Friendships have healthy ramifications for mankind. If you choose your friends poorly, you will be on your own when trouble happens. You will be abandoned, and abandonment is a lonely feeling. Abandonment causes emptiness. Emptiness is when the spirit leaves the body. When the spirit leaves, then man is dead.

Connections are made by two people having mutual likes and dislikes. Be very careful about who you stay connected to and why. Sin is expensive, and it is an easy trap. It is easy to become addicted to sin. Do not stay connected to a person that is morally corrupt, or they will corrupt you. Their bad morals will influence you and drag you down. It is in the nature of man to do as the people around him do. Guard yourself as if your life depended on it by choosing good friends. A good friend is one who loves their brother like their self.

Every man needs one best friend. A best friend will not abandon you. He will not turn his back or ignore you in your time of trouble. He will show up at anytime, anywhere, when you need him. A best friend is a lifetime friend. You will be at his funeral, or he will be at yours. If you do not have a friend like that at the end of your life, then you have likely chosen poorly.

A good way to make sure you have at least one very important person at your funeral is to make Jesus your best friend. Then you can legitimately claim that you will have a king at your funeral service. To be best friends with Jesus is to do like Jesus does and do like Jesus would have you do. Learn what Jesus did by reading your Bible. Study it for yourself to know the truth. Very importantly, do not "just take" my word for it. Doing that would be like having a friendship with somebody without ever meeting them, basically just being friends because I told you about him. That is ridiculous. Open the Bible yourself so that it can speak to you directly. You will make your own connections because Jesus's words are meant for you. Allow Jesus to be the leader in your life, and you will not be pulled any way depending on the day.

Having a relationship with Jesus is the most influential and important relationship in your life. Do not fail this part. I would argue that if you succeed here, then you will succeed in your other relationships too, solely on the strength of the positive influence Jesus will have over your life. And if you do not succeed in a relationship, then it is much easier to make meaning of the reasons why life happens as it does when you have an anchor point that does not change. The anchor point is Jesus. You change. I change. But Jesus does not. Furthermore, if a person is bad for you as a friend, they will scatter like cockroaches under the light of the gospel. The light of the gospel is Jesus. I heard one former drug addict call it the gos-pill. Everything was pills with this guy. Gos-pill. The message and person of Jesus is better than any drugs or pills. Gos-pill. Scientists have created their own little "replacements" in the form of pills, but none match the treating, healing, and freeing power of the message of the Gos-pill, the Gospel.

When you live a life that is guided by the message of the gospel, your life will speak for itself. You will not have to say a thing. It will be written in how you act and especially how you treat people. Bad friends will disappear. You will not have to be judgmental or point out their wrongdoings. You will simply be going in a different direction. The light of your spirit will illuminate the darkness in theirs, and without even realizing it, they will want to hide from you. Also, without even realizing it, people who are lost will be drawn to you.

Darkness is a description of that which is without light. Light pushes darkness out. Darkness is a synonym of evil. Evil is wickedness in the heart. Your heart can be drawn to evil, or it can be drawn away from evil. It all depends on who you spend your time with and where you choose to focus your attention. Did you know that if you place a painting in darkness that it will get darker? And did you know that if you place the same painting in light that it will get lighter? Darkness and light have the power to influence, persuade, and cause changes within.

My son, listen carefully. Just like you can perceive darkness and light with your eyes open, you can also perceive the dark and the light within a person with your spiritual eyes open. Your spiritual eyes get opened by reading your Bible and prayer.

Choose your friends with your eyes open!

Love,
Dad

LETTER 22

Dear Son,

Generosity is a position of the heart. In Hebrew, the oldest language, the word *heart* is pronounced lev. Lev has changed to love in English. Love is pronounced *AHaV* in Hebrew. The root word of love, very similar in pronunciation, *EHaV* implies I will give. To give is the root of generosity. Be generous, and God will be generous with you. The Bible says "to the measure you use so it will be used with you." When you die, your possessions will leave you forever, but what you give away will last forever. Generosity is a building block for your personal legacy. People will remember you much longer if you have a generous spirit than if you have a stingy spirit. You do not want to leave a legacy of stinginess. Generosity leaves a lasting impression. Stinginess makes you easy to be forgotten.

If you want to leave a legacy, leave it through love. Love is the root cause of generosity and charity. While love is not something to be expressed privately, generosity and charity are. Generosity and charity expressed publicly is advertisement. Advertise is what you do when you have something for sale. Man should not be for sale. God did not create man as merchandise to be sold. A man that is for sale cheapens himself. A man that causes others to be for sale is wicked. A man that is for sale is not a righteous man, and a man that buys other men is up to no good. Do not misconstrue this to say that buying a person's skill, work, or service means that you are up to no good. This is strictly talking about allowing yourself to be influenced or influencing others for the wrong (immoral) reasons. To say it more directly, Do not sell your soul to the devil or take part while others sell theirs to him.

Generosity is when you choose to put goodness out into the community. It is to give something away out of the kindness of your heart. Remember, everything you do is rooted in the disposition of your heart. Wherever your heart is, there is how you are led to be. If love is in your heart, you will be kind and generous with no expectation of a return. If deception is in your heart, you may be led to "act" kind and generous, but it will only be an act. To be and to act are very different. To be is who you are; it is a matter of your essence. To act is a matter of what your essence causes you to do. To put on an "act" is to pretend. To pretend is to create a false appearance, and that is what children do when they are playing.

These letters are written to teach you wisdom so that you will grow up and be a mature, righteous, and solid man. They are intended so that you will live a righteous and intentional life. They are written so that you will stop thinking as you did when you were a child and be a man.

Generosity is to give something away, to not hold back, and to put it all out there with no expectations of a return. The spirit of generosity is contagious. Being generous makes the community more peaceful. With peace comes prosperity and health. Look at the communities or countries with the least amount of peace. They take rather than give. They are ridden with war, drugs, crime, and violence. Those communities or countries are not at peace, and because they are not at peace, it makes prosperity impossible. Even worse, they are statistically less healthy where prosperity is missing. They do not live as long. Just make a quick comparison of the communities in America that are prosperous compared to those that are not prosperous, and you will see what I mean.

The law of reciprocity is at work when you are generous. Reciprocity is the subject of the nature of two people's relationship to each other. It is the substance that determines the outcome. Like nearly everything in your life, you get what you put in. If you take a lot, then much will be taken from you. If you put in a lot, you will be rewarded a lot. It is a biblical principle. *Principia* is also the Latin term for principle. Principia is the term for domain. You could also say that the term principle is under the domain of the Bible; its purpose is to teach you life principles. If you do this, then you will get this result. If you do A, then B will follow.

Being generous for the sake of being generous is health to the spirit. Generosity builds a man from the inside out. It gives you a strong, positive view of yourself, and it gives others a positive experience with you. It builds a bridge between you, the inner person, and the world outside of you. Generosity, as a way to be in your life, unites the two major religious philosophies of Judaism and Christianity. Jewish philosophy stressed the deeds and actions of man toward the world. Christian philosophy focuses on the internal heart of the man. God reaching out to man by the cross. As one preacher noted: the horizontal beam represents man's relationship to each other. The vertical beam represents man's relationship to God. Both are important and valuable. Both are necessary for the whole man and the whole human race. Generosity makes the world better right where you are.

It really does start with you.

Think of generosity like planting fruit trees in a spiritually barren land with spiritually hungry people. The world is filled with spiritually hungry people. There are those whose spirit is hungry for love, hungry for forgiveness (their guilt to go away), and those who are hungry for a break (those that are weary). The world needs you as an individual to pour out love generously. It needs you to give a piece of yourself and your stuff and your time to a person in need. It needs you to be a seed planter.

Have you ever noticed that with matters of nature God does not give nature a choice? Nature has its role written in to its genetic code. The fruit tree does not get a choice to produce fruit or not. Important fact: man was given the honor to choose. With choice comes responsibility. Responsibility comes with the big brain, soul, and spirit. Responsibility is the charge man was given when God bestowed dominion over the earth upon him. Because you have a choice on whether or not to plant seeds, there is no need to ask.

Just do it. Do it generously. My son, be kind to others, generously. Generosity is truly a bridge builder.

Give yourself, your stuff, and your time to others, and you will make the world, your world, a better place.

I have a hunch that your purpose stems in giving yourself away.

Love,
Dad

LETTER 23

Dear Son,

You must be content with what you have. Your joy is stolen when you do not learn to be content. Joy is one of the riches you were born with. It is in your heart. God bestowed it upon you as a part of your birthright. Your riches are your inheritance! You need only to find them, recognize them, and be thankful for them! It is a lie of the devil to tell you that there is anything in this world that you need to be content. Being content is a choice. Being content makes it easy to find joy.

Joy is directly affected by what you believe that you must possess in order to be content. You do not need anything that man made to have joy. Man only makes physical things. Joy is not a physical thing, yet you can possess it. It is man that wrongfully creates things and makes other men think those creations are necessary to have joy. Joy comes from inside of yourself. The stuff that man makes comes from outside of yourself. To believe you need any man-made thing to be content and thus possess joy is a lie.

Contentedness is a disposition of the heart. Your heart directly affects your beliefs. Your beliefs affect your choices. Your choices will make your life into whatever it is no matter which circumstances you are in.

You are in control of what matters to you and what does not matter to you. It is a matter of choice. You are in control of how much stuff you need to be content, or not. You can focus on what you have and be content, or you can focus on what you do not have and not be content. If you do not learn to be content, you will never find joy, and you will not be at peace. You get peace from being whole as a person. Wholeness is to be in tune with yourself and in tune with God simultaneously.

Your body is your temple. All of your riches are already inside of your temple. To be completely satisfied, you need only to invite God into your temple. God will illuminate your riches. Add God to the riches you were born with, and you will be completely whole. Wholeness brings peace. Satan will use any avenue possible to gain access to your temple. He will send countless salesmen to knock on your door in an attempt to get inside. They are merely solicitors. They will lie to you so that you wrongfully believe you must buy something outside your temple to be content. The spirit of discontent starts with believing Satan's solicitors.

They come in all forms, and they attempt to sell you all things. You need only to remember that there is not a single thing in the world that can completely satisfy you. Satisfaction begins with being content. It is a choice. You own the right to decide if you are content and what it takes for you to be content. Learning to be content does not mean that you give up working harder to improve your lot in life. Neither does it mean that you should not have dreams and goals and strive for them. Setting goals and working toward your goals is a sound biblical principle. God tells man, "You shall toil," and then He goes on to instruct man "to gain dominion over the earth." One is a goal. The other is work.

In very simple terms, He is saying, "Work hard and make a life for yourself." Make order on earth. Make order in your life. Make the world better for yourself, your family, and others. Use religion for right morals, structure, and discipline. Use science to improve lives and keep people alive. Religion and science are not at war. That is one of the lies from Satan's solicitors. It is perfectly good to use science, religion, and government to "gain dominion over the world." However, it must always be juxtaposed against a righteous disposition of the heart. A righteous disposition of the heart will keep your goals in check. It will keep you from cheating to win and causing harm to others because you want what they have. A righteous disposition is the root of being content because it gives you a right view of life.

Working hard is good, but making work central to your life is bad. Placing anything, other than God, as the centerpiece is the same as making an idol. The spirit of discontent will cause you to place work on the altar as an idol because the spirit of discontent causes you to wrongly look to the world to fill the missing piece. You cannot go to work and gain the missing piece nor can you work to earn the missing piece. It is not for sale. The missing piece is not of this world. The missing piece is God. The missing piece only comes when you invite Him in. It is a gift. When you invite Him in, you change your life in order to honor Him. The world will know it by how you act.

Only God can make you completely whole.

Being in union with God will help you to put your life in order. It gives you stability because you are tethered to an anchor point that does not change. Making God as the centerpiece is to make Him central in your life. That means you build your life around Him. It will cause you to have a right view of what is important and what is not. You will understand what it means to put first things first. The new, God-centered disposition in your heart will supernaturally change your entire disposition toward life. Your heart will be rightly disposed to the right things. You will learn to have gratitude for all the blessings God grants you on earth and all the riches that were bestowed upon you before earth.

Being content comes from having gratitude for what you possess. Having gratitude keeps your focus on what you do have rather than what you do not have. Focusing on what you do not have is the seed of discontent. It has caused many men to do immoral and foolish things to get what they want and do not have. It leads to disaster, and it will shackle you to your mistakes.

By not learning to be content, you also place yourself in a position to make stupid money decisions like buying something because your neighbor has it or because it is on sale.

Love,
Dad

LETTER 24

Dear Son,

Do not desecrate your temple. Do not desecrate or take part in desecrating the temple of another person. To desecrate is to abuse, violate, or contaminate that which is sacred. Your temple is sacred. Your temple is your body, soul, and spirit. They develop together from the time you were in your mother's womb. The view that your temple is sacred infers the highest value upon your being. It is the belief that the totality of your person is to be treated with the utmost respect. It is intended so that you will remain holy. In Hebrew, *holiness* means *separate*. Holiness is what gathers you near to God. Holiness makes you pure. Holiness happens when you are washed by the blood of Jesus.

Holiness goes much further than merely having good self-esteem. Self-esteem deals with the head; holiness deals with the heart. Modern man attributes everything to the head; the Bible attributes everything to the heart. Self-esteem is a modern psychological concept. It is the perception you have of your physical, psychological, and social attributes. To have good self-esteem is a good thing, but keep in mind that it goes through the filter of your life experiences and the disposition of your heart. The disposition in your heart is directly linked to your relationship to God. Your relationship to God is strengthened through your intentional choice to be holy.

You are made holy by acceptance of Jesus Christ as your Savior. His work on the cross makes you holy. You do not need to do anything else, but after you truly accept Him into your heart, you will change. With acceptance comes commitment. Commitment implies a willingness to work at the thing you are committed to. Accepting

Christ means you are obedient and plan to keep your temple sacred. God will only enter a holy temple. Your temple can be made holy through what? Yup, you said it: the washing of the Savior, Christ. The Holy Spirit enters your temple, and you are united to God. To be in unity with God is to be made whole. With wholeness comes peace in all seasons. With peace comes joy, also in all seasons.

By choosing to desecrate your temple, you are rejecting a relationship with God. By desecrating the temple of another person, you are also rejecting a relationship with God. Think of it like this. An artist paints the perfect painting. It is one of a kind, and it is priceless. If somebody ruins it, then it is irreplaceable. To be a part in desecrating it means that you take your paint brush and scissors and ruin it. Do you think you could have a relationship to the artist after ruining his work? Yet this is what happens every day; some person desecrates their own temple or takes part in desecrating another person's temple. Do not take part! Be ye separate! Taking part is to be complicit with. In legal terms, it means you are guilty too.

The sum of the Judaic Law is to love God with all your heart, mind, and soul and to love your brother as yourself. Desecrating your temple violates both because it rejects a relationship with God, which is the opposite of loving God. When you desecrate your own temple, it is because you do not have a high value of yourself. If the second part says to love your brother as yourself but you do not have a high value of yourself, then it is unlikely that you will have a high value of your brother.

Desecrating your temple happens when you live a life of sin with no boundaries. It is when you eat anything, look at anything, listen to anything, and do anything. With sin, anything goes. There are no boundaries and no rules. Where there are no rules, then there is chaos. Chaos is the antithesis of God because God is a God of order. You need only to look at the design of the world to see that there is order; the Designer created the world with order. When there is no order, there is anarchy. Where there is anarchy, there can be no peace. Where there is no peace, then there is no prosperity.

Your temple is the supreme creation on earth. It is designed to have multiple systems working in perfect harmony. It is perfectly ordered. It is meant to be cared for and treated with respect. A very crude explanation is to think of it like a supercomputer. It has hardware like your body. It has an operating system like your soul. It has the guy behind the buttons which is like your spirit. They are meant to work in conjunction with one another. The system itself is relatively safe until you open up a dangerous email, download infected software, or do not properly take care of the hardware.

One hundred percent of the time, your choices determine the outcome. Even if you lose, your choices determine how you lost; in that sense, you are cooperating with the world and with God to write your own story and be your own character in the story. Is your character a guy that spends hours looking at porn? How about looking at himself in the mirror? Is he a guy that says one thing and does another? Is he one that has no regard for his own personal health and wellness? Or does he only care about himself and nobody else? What kind of character in a novel does that? I'll tell you what kind, the bad guy.

The bad guy never wins at the end of the story. We, humans, know what kind of character it is in the story we are reading based on what they do. Why would your judgment of character be any different in real life? Why would it change when judging yourself? You use the same character gauge to determine both. In fact, the same gauge you use to distinguish goodness or badness for a character in somebody else's novel is the gauge you should use for yourself.

Furthermore, the same gauge you use to determine good and bad, good and evil, or right and wrong is the gauge you need to use when asking whether the thing you are doing desecrates your temple. If you are hiding it from others, then it's probably a form of desecration. If you lie about it, then it's probably a form of desecration. If you have to sneak around to do it, then it is desecration. And if the Bible says it is wrong, then you better listen because unlike all the other modern psychology theories that have come and gone, the Bible has withstood the test of time.

Love,
Dad

LETTER 25

Dear Son,

America is just worried about cosmetics. It views what is on the outside more important than what is on the inside. It has shifted man's intrinsic value from substance to social status. We have even begun to diagnose man's problems wrongly. American (western) psychology places man's problems in the head. The Bible places man's problems in the heart. The two yield very different starting points and thus two very different ends for the human predicament. How can we come up with the right answer if we do not even ask the right question? With two vastly different starting points, there is no wonder how we come up with two vastly different ending points. The heart is in the body. The head guides the body. The head is Christ. The body is the church. The irony is that man blamed the head, Christ, and therefore killed Him. When He beat death, men blamed the church instead. The analogy is obvious: modern man, like his ancestors, blames the head of the church, Jesus, and when it is unable to fix man's problems by changing the head, Jesus, then it blames the body, which is the church. Remember, the church is made up of you and others like you as believers in Christ, no matter how strong or weak you are in your involvement.

The Bible is correct here because the problem is rightly found in the heart. This is my second letter to you concerning the heart. Get this part right, and your life will go well no matter your circumstances. Fail here, and it will not matter who you marry, how much money you make, what your social status is, or any other thing you can think of to add to your life; none will matter. They are all merely furniture in an empty temple. If your heart is wrong, you will not have peace or know joy. Cosmetics can only dress a thing up. In fact, if you put too much cosmetics on a thing, it makes it look obviously gaudy and atrocious. Cosmetics are merely a dressing that will show themselves for what they are over time. Imagine using a spray can over rusty metal. It may look good for a day, but the rust will eat its way through and destroy the metal. The heart is like the metal. It is the deepest, innermost private part of a person. The heart is deceitful above all things and dispiritedly wicked (Jeremiah 17:9–10).

The rust attacks the innermost part of the metal. Sin is like the rust; it attacks the deepest most inner part of the person. The outer part of a person can be dressed up just as the rust can be painted over. The truth of the quality within the substance always bleeds its way through. It destroys from the inside so that you can see it on the outside. It comes through the cosmetics and shows itself for what it is.

Just look to Hollywood, and you will see my point. From the outside, celebrities appear to live the perfect life. Some make more money than an entire ZIP code, and their houses cost more than several city blocks. Everything that a person is able to buy is at their fingertips, yet they do not have peace or joy. They are empty temples, and their belly is never satisfied. It is because they have bought into the lie that what is on the outside is more important than what is on the inside. They choose their friends based on power and success. They waste their time, energy, and money in a fickle attempt to make life better by changing the conditions externally without changing the conditions internally.

If you change the conditions internally, it will not matter what happens externally because you will be able to handle any circumstance. To have the right conditions internally, you must have a right disposition.

Your disposition is born out of which god you choose to serve. You do not serve God by building big houses or driving a nice car. You serve God by devoting the stuff you cannot buy like time, love, faithfulness, and personal sacrifice to building His kingdom. Building His kingdom is not a public relations event nor is it motivated by politics. Love and faithfulness are the only motives. Pride and personal gain are not the right motives. Building God's kingdom is personal because it comes from a person, and it is meant for a person. It is buttressed by relationships between people. If there is a person that is doing a deed with the wrong motives, then it is like the metal being infected by rust. It is cancer to the community and directly affects the order of God's design.

Do not be that guy.

In the same way, the interior of the metal cannot just be hidden under new paint if it is compromised; you cannot dress up poor character with nice clothes, fake eyelashes, or silicon. When you pick your wife, make sure her character matches her looks, and you will have chosen well. She will get more beautiful as she ages. If you pick her solely for her fake looks, just remember that you will have to wake up next to her when she is not wearing makeup, and with poor character, she will grow uglier on you much faster.

There are qualities that are attractive which flow from the heart. You will notice those in others, and you will judge others according to those qualities or lack thereof. Be aware that you will be judged by those same intrinsic qualities.

Who you are in your heart is where the most attractive and constructive qualities that you possess come from. Who you are in your heart is also where the most unattractive and destructive qualities come from. Your soul always has a choice on which way you will be. Concerning yourself primarily with the flesh is analogous to using the spray can on rusted metal. If you want change then start with the heart. The heart cannot be mastered without the intervention of a supernatural, holy God. Jesus is the only "transformer." You cannot do it yourself, and you cannot do it with a man-made, lifeless god like money, car, house, or improved looks. In the same way, man cannot help a caterpillar become a butterfly because the pattern for its transformation is intrinsic: it comes from God; man cannot help man transform his own heart without the pattern from God. The pattern is Jesus Christ.

Save yourself a lot of wasted time, heartache, and headache by listening to me. It is foolish to think mere cosmetics will do. Cosmetics are akin to taping wings on the caterpillar and thinking it will fly.

Love,
Dad

LETTER 26

Dear Son,

When you give something in your life to God then really do give it to Him. Giving something away means that it is no longer yours. It means that you do not possess rights over it; therefore, you are no longer in control. If you give something to God, then it is God's to do with as He chooses. Do not keep controlling interest for yourself while claiming you have given it to God.

It's no wonder so many prayers go unanswered. I imagine they go something like this: "God, please fix this; I'm giving this to you. It is yours." God responds, "But wait a second. It's not mine. It's still yours. You have controlling interest. Fix it yourself." Giving God controlling interest is to hand over the rights, take your hand off the wheel, and allowing God time to do it while having faith that He will.

It is in the nature of man to be a busy body, to reject rest. Oftentimes, busyness is just mindless motion. To focus the hands without focusing the mind is simply to be busy without really focusing. It's folding laundry, wiping down the dashboard in your car, or playing solitaire on the computer. Conversely, prayer like any good conversation is engaging and focused. A solid prayer life is the foundation of your relationship with God. Steady prayer is like steadily placing money in the savings account. It will bring you peace and security in your future. The key is that you place it and leave it. Most importantly, do not touch it. Do not interject your busy little hands in to the mix.

If you know an investor that can predict the market with one hundred percent accuracy every time but you had to trust in his timing along with his knowledge to predict, would you hand him your money then get it back a day later because you are too anxious to wait? Would that be wise? Is that a good move? Could you really do more with it than an investor with a one hundred percent accurate prediction rate? Could you do more than you have already done? Then why is it a mess in the first place?

But we do this all the time with our prayers. We say we've given it to God but refuse to wait for God. Rather than giving it to God and then showing our faith by getting out of God's way, we "say" we've given it to God and then get right back in the way. Lack of faith is always proved by impatience. If you are impatient because God did not answer your prayer "right now," you must get out of your westernized, want-it-right-now mentality. I call it the fast-food mindset. More importantly, remember that the teacher is always silent during the test.

God put the pieces together to make an entire universe out of nothing. He physically created something out of nothing. He can move the pieces to fit so that even down to the atomic level, all can be rearranged, including that mess you don't know how to fix. Just as some molecules need different catalysts to break down and each break down period requires a different amount of time and energy, so also your mess has its own time and way to be fixed. Wisdom is letting time be a part of the equation. Time is the best detergent. It is very difficult to master because it literally means hands off. It is to place your prayer at the footstool of God, leave it there, and do not touch it again no matter the amount of time it takes for an answer.

Mastering this sort of spiritual discipline is the apex of understanding who God is and His order of operation. It is the culmination of your spiritual maturity. It takes daily practice at resistance to your own will. It is called submission.

It also takes faith in God. Faith is belief in that which you do not see. Faith starts out tiny and grows slower than a redwood. When it grows big, then people can see it from a long way off. It towers over every other living thing. Yes, faith is a living thing (not in the naturalistic, organic way) in the sense that it grows, pumped to life by the spirit of God. Faith will see you through the storm. Just like a redwood, strong faith will still be standing after the storm. The storm helps it by pruning the weakest limbs so that the stronger limbs can get more nutrients. More life. In turn, growing stronger and bigger. As it grows, then it becomes a more vital part of its local ecosystem providing protection for smaller weaker trees and safety for wildlife.

As you learn to pray, you will naturally grow in your relationship with God. The more your relationship with any person grows, the more you learn about that person. As you learn more about God through your relationship with Him, your faith will grow. You will see God and all His attributes as they work themselves out in your life. When faith grows, it matures. When you develop that type of mature faith, then you will be a living tower just like a redwood.

P.S. You ain't going to get somewhere by just sitting there. And you ain't going to get to a destination by going the wrong way.

Love,
Dad

LETTER 27

Dear Son,

If you do not listen, God will send His hound to hound you until you do. There is no distance the Lord will not go to get you back. Just think how many people that we, humans, bring to the scene when a child has wondered off and gets lost—tens, sometimes hundreds, and even thousands. We show up with K9s, and we put out alerts with the child's face on it. Every person in the country is on high alert and looking for the lost child. Do you not think that God does not do the same? No doubt the angels are on high alert when one of God's children wanders off. God sets out roadblocks and siren calls to get His children back. He sends His hound to find you. I want you to understand this eternal truth: God loves you, and there is no bounds that will keep Him from getting to the pit of your heart to bring you home.

There is something in all men that causes them to search the world for the thing it offers. They go out searching with the belief that the thing to satisfy their self, the magic key, comes from the world. It is partly because there is a need to fill an empty pit in their heart, and it is partly because there is a need to make meaning out of their life. To be satisfied, you must feel as if your life has meaning. It is inside you to want a meaningful life because it is inside you to know that life has value. Value is a by-product of the moral law. It is a built-in guidepost. The moral law is how you are able to distinguish between good or bad, right or wrong, and righteousness and unrighteousness.

Men are dangerous. They are capable of destroying millions and millions of their kind. Can you imagine a lion killing millions of other lions in the jungle? How about an ant? Because God gave man such capabilities, He also gave man the moral law. It is what keeps men from destroying each other and it is necessary so that men can live peaceably. Remember, without peace, there is no prosperity. Prosperity is to have internal and external riches. Internal riches are riches that you are born with like peace, joy, and the ability to love. Internal riches happen inside of you. External riches come from outside of you. Internal riches need always come first. Unless you gain internal riches first, external riches will not satisfy you. External riches without internal riches is not complete prosperity. Complete prosperity leads to true prosperity. True prosperity is built on the foundation of truth about whether or not you are fulfilling your purpose. It is to be internally and externally prosperous while also fulfilling your purpose. You will feel like you are living your best life when you are fulfilling your purpose. And I imagine you will also feel richer than you ever felt.

By the world's standard, being rich is to be a millionaire, and being a millionaire will make you happy. There are countless unhappy millionaires. Happiness depends on what's happening. Joy comes from the wellspring within. The devil deceives you by tricking you into believing that you will be satisfied from something this world has to offer. That is what causes you to search and still be wanting, not filled. That is what causes you to be thrown off course by magnets—to lose your True North and become lost. That is why God will send His hounds to find you.

To lust for something is to want something *right now*. It is to be unable to wait for it. Sin is the outworking of lust working inside the heart. Sin inevitably leads to slavery. Ironically, at the beginning of a sinful path, the sinner defends the sin. It is as if they have Stockholm Syndrome. Stockholm Syndrome is when a person that gets kidnapped defends their kidnapper. It is when the perspective gets distorted. Sin is the kidnapper.

The Hound of Heaven will not bite you and drag you home. He will find you and bark at you and frustrate your plans until you get to the end of yourself and choose to come home on your own. Then He will walk you home. Son, hear these words: the walk home is always a long, lonely walk. It is good to be humbled in life. You gain clarity with a heart of humility. Pride, ego, and arrogance always get in the way of perception. It is admirable to be wrong and admit that you are wrong. It is dangerous to ignore it and deadly to continue.

The Bible has treasures of revelation that are oceans deep. At the surface level, the revelation is simple: BIBLE—basic instructions before leaving earth. The surface revelation is that the Bible is meant to be a light for mankind so that you can walk a right path. Jesus is the light. Keep the light near and it is easier to see physical and spiritual dangers and pitfalls. Take the light away and the danger goes up exponentially. Think of it like this: There will always be danger in a fallen world. There is danger on the savanna during the day, but it is much more dangerous and scarier at night. It is not necessary to elaborate on all the dangers. The point is that you can see much clearer when you have light to illuminate your surroundings.

The Bible likens sin to darkness, filth, and squalor. Living in sin is living in darkness. What would happen if you lived in utter darkness with no daylight and no electricity or night lights to take showers, do daily tasks, make your meals, or clean up after yourself? You would make a mess of your life. If anybody lived with you, you would probably bump into them and knock them down and hurt them. Imagine you lived like this for three years or five? You might pick up a lot of survival habits, most of which you probably would not do if you had the lights on. You would be guarded and unsure of yourself. Now after five years, the lights come back on. Can you imagine what a wreck everything in your life would be? Everything would be in disrepair. Even the lives of the people around you would have been affected by it. It would take a long time to get it all back in order. You'd probably still be unsure, and you would definitely have to practice undoing some of your bad habits.

The Hound of Heaven will bother you until you come back home. That's how God has set it up. That's his job. When you get to the end of yourself and decide to come back home, be patient because it will take time to get your life back in order. Most importantly, I promise you will be so thankful for the light.

Love,
Dad

LETTER 28

Dear Son,

All of these letters are not meant to replace the Bible. They can't. They are strictly meant to build on some of the core principles and wisdom of the Bible. They are intended to get you thinking about your beliefs by challenging the wrong ones and giving you a good reason to keep the right ones. Hopefully, they will be seeds that cause you to be curious and read the gospel yourself. I call it the Gos-Pill. It is the medication you should use first when you need to be healed. The philosophical truth within the Bible is irreplaceable. The heart of the gospel is salvation, and the theme of the gospel is transformation. It is intended to transform a life from the inside out, from the heart. Remember, when a person's thinking is faulty, they need to start with the heart. The heart shapes the beliefs, and the beliefs are what make you do what you do.

Religion for structure and learning is a good thing, but be careful because religion may lead to pride. Religion is what the Pharisees had. Religion (going to church, saying the rosary, acting pious, and even fasting) in itself is not the answer. The answer is to accept Christ as your necessary Savior and then give Him lordship over your life by allowing Him to be your guiding light. By accepting Him as your Savior, your sins are redeemed, paid for. By calling Him Lord, you are giving Him authority over your life. He said I love you enough to give My life for you, and you respond by accepting it and giving your life back to Him. It is the perfect picture of a marriage—a sanctified commitment to a relationship by two persons.

Ideally, the religious aspect—prayer, fasting, study, and thinking about God—are meant so that you can be your best when things go bad. The Christian theologian Oswald Chambers put it this way: "Obey the spirit of God. Practice what God has put in your heart by His spirit and when crisis comes your nature will prevail." They (whoever they are) say it takes ten thousand hours to gain mastery over something. Character building also takes ten thousand hours to master, except it only takes a few seconds (one decision) to start back at hour one. The seeds of good character may be planted by a good teacher at a young age, and they may be cultivated and reinforced along the way, but good character can only be validated after years of consistent proof. You don't get that designation for holding the door for the elderly lady "that one time." And you certainly don't get it because you have good looks, a good job, or come from a good family. Character is something you have to earn regardless of your name, title, or circumstances. People recognize your good character because you do the right thing when everybody is looking and when nobody is looking, and you've consistently done that for a long time. You get that designation when you don't talk about people behind their back and when you treat people lower than you like they are equal. You keep that designation by doing the hard thing when it would be easier to take the easy road.

At its core, the Bible teaches you to have good character. What do you find in the core of an apple? Seeds, right? Seeds that will become plants that will produce more fruit. If every person in a society has good character, there would be less laws. When the constitution was written, it was assumed that the country would remain a God-fearing, moral country. That's why the constitution focuses on liberty rather than laws. Have you noticed that the further away from God this country gets, the more laws we create to keep men within the boundaries? If all people had good character, then men would live peaceably without laws. The lawmakers are just as corrupt as the lawbreakers. Utopia is only possible if every single person has good character. But since all men have evil in their heart, a utopian society on earth is impossible. The wisest thing is to look forward to heaven as the final answer for man to live in a utopia.

I'm not sure having a meaningful life would be so clear if life was easy and the world was perfect. Meaning gets clearer after pain.

Pain is a counter balance to pleasure. Going through pain is a test of character. Good character does the right thing under duress and discomfort. Conversely, it is tempered with humility when life seems grand. Bad character will cause you to create a life that you hate because you alienate yourself from others for the simple reason that nobody wants to be around a person with bad character. Your life will suck because, externally, the thing that brings happiness is the people.

A celebration is not a celebration without the people. People are what make life interesting and colorful. There are lots of studies that show having healthy relationships improve health and happiness of a person. Remember, happiness is tied to what's happening. It is temporary. Joy comes from within.

There are many moving parts that are intertwined and connected in your life. Morals and meaning are connected to nearly everything in your life. In his feebleness, man (including me, I suppose) has attempted to disentangle morals from meaning. Beware, morals and meaning come from God. It would take me a series of books to explain it, but they are not meant to be pulled apart. The best way is to choose to live a morally good life so that you maintain more control over the meaning. This is not to say that one causes the other. It simply means that it is easier to guide your own life when you do the right thing.

As you know, I am writing these letters from inside of a federal prison cell. It is only six by ten square feet. It's February, and the concrete is cold, maybe fifty degrees. The window is missing a bottom row of panes, and there is a sliding piece of plastic to cover the missing pieces. The cold wind refuses to stay out. I have a double bunk bed with no bunkie. My locker is half-full. There are six small shelves inside. Two have clothes, two have books and writing tablets, one has hygiene and shower stuff, one has coffee, a cup, and a few tunas. I have so little, but I have so much. By taking me to the bottom board, God has revealed where my riches are. Having so little has allowed me to think about what it really is to have much in life, what true riches are, life and its meaning, and other things that are very important for living a fulfilling life.

I watch as some of the staff come and go and never seem satisfied with their own lives. I watch as men get released to the free world scared and unsure of themselves. I watch as others leave with a plan that can only lead them back. I am at a medical center where men come for dialysis, surgeries, and other types of high-level medical care. I watch as guys on dialysis get their limbs cut off. Some leave one limb at a time until the only parts left are the most essentially necessary to stay alive. From my perspective, it appears like it hurts just to stay alive. There is one friend of mine who is more thankful to be alive than people who are in much better physical shape. There are many, many people here missing arms and legs. One recently asked me to pray for him because he is fighting a yearlong foot infection that doctors say will be amputated. He was once six foot three inches tall and built like a college football player. Now he is reduced to a wheelchair and bandages. His eyes show the story of a broken man. Men from all over the country come here each year to die. I hear their stories, and they have been gone for two, three, even four, and five decades. Their families have long forgotten about them. Society has forgotten about them. They are the ones that Jesus is speaking about when he says, "I was in prison, and you did not come to see me." Despite having access to a phone and computers, many do not have a person to contact. It has caused me to be all the more thankful for my own wellness and health. It has caused me to value my wife and children all the more.

I have fallen in love with Julie even more without being able to touch her. The best advice I can give you regarding your personal relationships is this: When you got gold, you better know it.

A father's job is to pass down wisdom to his children. These letters are my attempt to write for you what I am not there to show you. I'm sorry for neglecting my duty to you as a dad. Nothing I do will ever bring back the fifteen years I have been gone over the course of your life. They won't place me there for your triumphal moments in life nor will they place me there when you needed me to hug you, build you up, or correct you to keep you on the right path. When I began these letters, I just wanted to write simple, valuable advice for you—stuff that has taken me forty years wandering in the wilderness to figure out, stuff that I had to learn the hard way. I have backed them up with a ton of prayer for you. Ultimately, it will be up to you to figure it out for yourself. To think through your own life, enjoy the good times, deal with the pain, and make meaning of it all. My heart is with you. I want you to be the best version of yourself. I want you to be content and satisfied and filled with joy. I want you to make the most of your tools and find true riches. I want you to be a good man. I want you to come forth in front of God pure as gold. May these words bless you and keep you and never leave you. Most of all, may God's face shines upon you, and may His presence guides you with the light of His glory.

Love,
Dad

About the Author

Vincent graduated from the University of Missouri, Kansas City. He lives in Missouri with his family.